a
single
life
to live

a single life to live

STOP WAITING FOR YOUR LIFE TO BEGIN
AND THRIVE WHERE GOD HAS YOU TODAY

HANNAH SCHERMERHORN

BakerBooks

a division of Baker Publishing Group
Grand Rapids, Michigan

Published by Baker Books
a division of Baker Publishing Group
PO Box 6287, Grand Rapids, MI 49516-6287
www.bakerbooks.com

Printed in the United States of America

Library of Congress Cataloging-in-Publication Data
Names: Schermerhorn, Hannah, 1992- author.
Title: A single life to live : stop waiting for your life to begin and thrive where God has you today / Hannah Schermerhorn.
Description: Grand Rapids, MI : Baker Books, a division of Baker Publishing Group, [2023] | Includes bibliographical references.
Identifiers: LCCN 2022023116 | ISBN 9781540902733 (paperback) | ISBN 9781540903075 (casebound) | ISBN 9781493439621 (ebook)
Subjects: LCSH: Single people—Religious life. | Christian life.
Classification: LCC BV4596.S5 S34 2023 | DDC 204/.408652—dc23/eng/20220706
LC record available at https://lccn.loc.gov/2022023116

The author is represented by the literary agency of Jones Literary, LLC.

Baker Publishing Group publications use paper produced from sustainable forestry practices and post-consumer waste whenever possible.

23   24   25   26   27   28   29   7   6   5   4   3   2   1

To Penny, Jack, Otto, and Tessa Schermerhorn.
And to Kazu and Ruah Treuden.
May you always know
how much God truly loves you.

contents

introduction

B-TEAM

Being single can feel a lot like being picked for the B-Team. The A-Team (aka your married friends) are celebrated people. Beautiful parties are thrown with presents and fancy dresses when they get engaged and married. Everyone loves their cute couple photos that are plastered all over social media. They are leaders at work and in church. They are admired by their community, and children hope to grow up to be just like them.

But what is left for the B-Team? All we get are pitied looks from friends and family when we go by ourselves to the weddings and celebrations for the A-Team. At work we are easily chosen for the extra projects and late nights because we do not have a family to go home to. At church we are given all the tasks and service projects other people do not want because we are "blessed with so much free time in our singleness."

At some point, everyone in our lives decides that they need to help us get promoted from the B-Team to the A-Team. Conversations then turn from things we care and dream about to the only acceptable topic of conversation—"Who are you dating?" and "I know this great person I think you should date."

Being on the B-Team can be exhausting. But what shatters my heart even more is that I never wanted to be on the B-Team in the first place.

I thought I was going to grow up, get married, and live happily ever after. I even thought I had made it onto the A-Team. I had the beautiful engagement ring, the specially chosen wedding dress, and a man I was thrilled to be marrying.

Unfortunately, just a few months before my wedding was supposed to take place, Satan stepped in and caused enough destruction to end my engagement. My wedding was canceled. My relationship was over. The chalkboard with all my plans and dreams for the future was erased, and I was full of anxiety, depression, and overwhelming disappointment that I was once again stuck on the B-Team.

I have been single for six years since that horrible day and have found myself in some pretty dark places. At my best, I tried everything to end my singleness—from going on set-ups to praying to always looking my best when I went out in case I happened to run into the right guy. At my worst, I have lain on the floor with tears streaming down my face, begging God to just let me go to heaven because I was so sick of living a life I never wanted.

I have struggled with so many parts of singleness:

- Feeling like I have done something wrong to still be single
- Wishing I could just be happy like everyone else
- Asking, "If God loves me, why is He letting this be the reality of my life?"
- Wondering if I will ever get married and have kids like I have always longed for
- Feeling tired of being the third wheel

- Growing sick of spending free time alone
- Wishing I had a significant other to share news with, help with my problems, and truly understand me
- Harboring jealousy for friends' relationships
- Waiting for life to begin at marriage
- Feeling angry and untrusting toward God for allowing me to suffer alone for so long

The bullets could go on and on.

Have you felt any of those emotions? Have you asked yourself any of those questions? If so, can I tell you something that I have been learning?

In all my struggles, in all my pain, God has been guiding me to a realization that could change my entire life.

Right here and now in my singleness, God is offering me a life of true fulfillment and love that could completely overwhelm me and gently wrap me up. It is a life full of purpose in discovering how I am uniquely designed. It is a life where I can wake up in the morning and be exhilarated with what the day will bring. And it is up to me to either ignore it and chase after my own ideas of happiness (which clearly is not working) or embrace what God is offering.

You know what the best part of that life is? God is not just offering it to me. He is offering the same beautiful life to you, my friend. You and I have the choice to embrace it every single day.

I understand if you are skeptical. I have been sitting on the B-Team for a long time, and I know that finding joy in singleness can feel like trying to find a missing contact lens or the Loch Ness Monster. But I have started to take steps on this path, and I am already amazed with what I've found.

Are you ready to join me? I promise that if you go on this journey with me to find that beautiful life, you will not be disappointed. But I must warn you right now, if you say yes to going down that path, God is most likely going to greatly exceed your expectations like He has already done for me.

If you are ready, in these pages we will explore stories of the many bachelors and bachelorettes in the Bible and see how aspects of their lives apply to modern singleness. I am going to share my story of singleness and why I struggled for so long. We are going to wrestle with our own lives, hopes, and disappointments in order to arrive in the beautiful destination that God has made for us to enjoy.

To make the most out of these pages, here are two recommendations:

1. Grab a journal. Many of the chapters have little quizzes and activities to work through. If you are like me and do not like writing in books (except to highlight favorite quotes), a journal will be a great place for you to work through these exercises, along with any other thoughts you have as you read this book. Also, at the end of each chapter there are questions to help you apply the content. You can record your thoughts, observations, and answers, then pray about them or discuss them at brunch with other friends who are reading this book.

2. Consider counseling. We are going to unpack some big and heavy topics. I promise there will also be light and fun parts, but I am going to ask you to challenge yourself and think about some uncomfortable things. You do not need to do that alone. Counseling is a wonderful way to work through these subjects so you can continue to grow and thrive. In fact, the reason I can share most of the information in this book is because a counselor helped me through it all first.

That's it! Are you ready to see what God has in store for you? Let's dive into these pages to discover the truth: Happily ever after does not begin with marriage. It begins right now.

1

identity

MY FRIEND, I do not know your story. I do not know if you have been single for many years like me or if you have recently gone through a heartbreak. I wish I could grab coffee with you and understand all the pain and disappointment you have gone through in your singleness. I would love to hear about your scars and let you know how much I admire you for who you are right now and how you continue to show up in a life you had not planned.

Your pain does not scare me, and the questions you are afraid to admit to anyone live in my head as well. Questions like, "What is wrong with me that I am single?" "Does God not care about me?" "Have I done something wrong to be single?" "Will I be single for the rest of my life?"

These questions—along with so many more—rumble through my mind much more frequently than I would like to admit. Sometimes I do not see them for many weeks. Other times they are waiting for me when I wake up, follow me throughout the day, and haunt me at night when I cannot sleep.

These unwelcomed questions run through my head quite often, but there is one overarching question that always pops into my mind: "How did my life turn out this way?" Being single was never the plan.

When you were a kid, did you dream of what your "happily ever after" adult life would look like? Maybe you imagined how you would meet your significant other while traveling abroad. You would be lost and bump into this local who would help you and then give you a majestic tour of the city. As you connected deeply, you would find out they were a Christian millionaire who volunteers to help orphans. You would fall in love, get married, and have a social media perfect life together. Or maybe you had a more realistic, vague idea of being happily married by now, perhaps with a few kids running around.

How do you feel as you look at your life compared with that dream? Like mine, does your heart fill with sadness as you realize that your actual life could not be more opposite to the one your younger self imagined?

Sometimes I ask myself what the younger version of me would think if she met me now. No husband, no kids, not even an eligible prospect to date in sight. I am single, and the only running around in my house is my cat chasing an avocado toy filled with catnip. I never expected my life to turn out this way.

So how did you and I get to this "single" point in our lives? Especially when we had hoped and planned for a very different life. And why do we have to live this way, especially if we do not want to? Over the past six years God has been showing me the answers to all those questions. He has been opening my eyes to the wonderful possibilities of this single life, and I am hoping that you will be able to experience the joy of singleness with me. But the journey to get to this place has not always been smooth. It has been full of crushed hopes, exposed fears, and plenty of questions for God. So let's start at the very beginning.

BECOMING SINGLE

This is not an easy story for me to share. People I have known for years have not heard it. Sometimes if I am sipping wine, I can get through it without crying, but normally the tears come out as I share this. But I trust you, and sharing my story is the first step to walking toward our beautiful destination together. A destination where we can be more than just content in our singleness. We can be truly thrilled with our lives.

So here I go (gulp).

My story began in college. In my freshman year, I met a guy who seemed to check most of the boxes on the ridiculous list of what I wanted in a boyfriend. Thankfully I no longer have that list and cannot embarrass myself by sharing dating expectations of freshman Hannah (having a British accent may or may not have been one of them). I do know that some of the more *realistic* items on the list included being smart, kind, cute, and deeply passionate about his faith.

I had a crush on this guy for months. Of course, he liked someone else, so I went to every event I knew he would be at, tried to have normal, nonawkward conversations with him, and begged God to make him like me. Eventually it worked (but please do not take my life as a dating formula).

When we started dating, I was thrilled. I had never fallen in love before, and it was an emotional roller coaster that I loved being on. Holding hands, taking late-night walks with deep conversations, making dinner together, having someone who cared about the mundane details of my life, having someone to hug when I was (always) stressed out, and having someone who loved me filled me with happiness. It was not all sunshine and rainbows though. There were also plenty of tears and fights as we figured out how to make our independent lives work together.

But eventually, after three years of working to align on every belief and detail of our hopes for the future, we decided we were ready to take the next step into marriage. One beautiful, sunny vacation day on a Florida beach, I got the custom-designed engagement ring and was ecstatic about the next chapter of my life. I could not believe that things was turning out just like I had always hoped. We planned when we would get married, where we would work, where we would live, and how many kids we would have. We booked our venue, told our friends and family the wedding date, met the photographer, chose the color palette, and ordered the dresses.

But then we got a package in the mail. It contained two little booklets from our photographer. There was a "his" booklet and a "hers" booklet of "How well do I know my fiancé/fiancée?"

I thought I would get every question right. I thought we had talked through every detail of each other's lives, but I was wrong. Most of the pages were filled with lighthearted questions like, "What is their favorite color?" or "What is their favorite movie?" But on one of the pages in my booklet, there was a particularly serious question. It asked, "Has he gotten over an addiction?"

I felt pride as I answered the question. You see, when we had first started dating, my fiancé and I had put in some relationship work after he, heartbroken, admitted to me his struggle with addiction. He hated it, my heart felt for him, and we worked through books, went to counseling, did some soul searching,—everything we could find to get him through it. By our third year of dating, I thought the addiction had been gone for a long time. But the problem with addiction, I learned, is that it can come back with a vengeance.

So when I told him the answer to "Has he gotten over an addiction?" was yes with a big smile on my face, he admitted that the answer was actually no. The addiction had come back, and he had been struggling deeply for the past few months without my knowledge.

I have never experienced anything close to the depth of the sinking feeling I had in that moment. I dealt with his addiction in dating, and I knew it would break me in marriage. From the truth of a small booklet, my life suddenly shifted as I realized the future would not match the beautiful picture I had imagined. My dreams shattered as my confidence in our relationship was broken. I felt betrayed. I felt so naive. I even struggled with blaming myself for causing his relapse. I was furious and heartbroken and wrestled with what to do. Why was this happening to us? I lost it. I sobbed and went home without saying a word to him.

I want to pause here and say something very important. If you are dealing with an addiction or have dealt with one in the past, you are not unlovable, and you are not unworthy. A counselor would be much better help than I, but if you stick with me through the full story of this book, I will also share the parts of my story that tell you how truly valuable you are. I pray that this small piece of my story does not make you judge yourself in a negative way, because that is not in any way my intent.

After he admitted his relapse to me, we tried to make our relationship work for a couple of months. There were so many conversations where I tried to give back my ring and he would not take it, promising not to let his addiction hurt me again. But Satan kept on pushing at him, and it would be only a few days or weeks until we had to have the same tear-filled conversation again.

The hardest part was that I did not know what to do. Should I keep fighting with and for someone I loved, or should I give up on him, and then what would happen to him? I knew he was a good person, just someone who had a sin that overtook him, like all human beings experience.

The struggle to figure out what to do allowed my anxiety to take control of me, which spiraled me toward depression, panic attacks, and a complete numbness to life. My fiancé and I tried more counseling. We tried taking breaks. But nothing was solving our problem. Meanwhile, apparently we looked totally fine as a couple to bystanders. People would tell me how excited they were for my wedding, and I would try to respond without crying. It made the entire situation hurt even more.

Eventually God made the choice of what to do very clear for me. One day, "after a break," my fiancé and I were eating lunch and talking. My memory of that conversation is that it was my fault that our situation had turned out the way it had. Other girls would be accepting of his addiction, and it was my fault that I was not. Once that was established, I grabbed my stuff and walked out of his room, knowing that our relationship was over for good.

After I walked out, adrenaline was pumping through me, so I naturally decided to go to class. I acted normal, laughed at jokes, and answered questions as if my world had not just changed. It was not until I was home alone at night that it all hit me. I thought I had done everything right to find my significant other. I thought I had found my person and would never have to search again, but to my horror, I realized this was not true. Every single piece of me loathed the fact that I was once again single. It felt like a prison sentence.

THE STAGES OF SINGLENESS

In the time since that first dreaded day of singleness, I have struggled with so many aspects of being single. The first difficulty was the post-breakup phase. Obviously having an unused wedding dress in my closet continuously reminded me of how my plans and hopes had been crushed. Then there were the smaller things I did not expect. The first time I had exciting news after the breakup, I eagerly pulled out my phone to tell my ex only to realize that he was no longer the person I could talk to about things. It was just me now. I desperately missed companionship and simple things like having someone to converse with each day.

I had no desire to date again, but my sadness was combined with jealousy as my friends' own love stories began and blossomed into marriage. I hoped my fake "congratulations!" smile would conceal my overwhelming jealousy. At the umpteenth wedding RSVP of marking "no guest," I wondered, *What did all these other people do to get the life I have always wanted? Am I being punished for something?*

Next came the "it's time to start dating again" phase. Society decided that my relationship mourning phase was over, and I needed to get back into the dating game. Kind humans in my life grew excited as they schemed setting me up with any eligible bachelor they could think of (even if it was my "great-aunt's ferret-sitter's dentist").

It took me almost a year after my breakup to feel comfortable trying to date again. Of course, going on dates was easy. All I had to do was put on a fake smile and pretend that I had my life together to impress someone I was meeting for the first time in order to see if we would spend the rest of our lives together. Walk in the park, right? I hated it.

I would agree to go on dates and then stupidly get my hopes up as I heard how amazing my great-aunt's ferret-sitter's dentist was. It normally took only a few dates (if not a few minutes of a date) to realize that I should not have let myself be excited about the person—"No, I'm not getting tattoos over every inch of my body." "No, I don't want to learn how to do taxidermy." "No, I'm not going to quit my job to raise baby tarantulas with you." (OK, none of those were the real reasons, but you get the point.) I despaired that all the good people were already taken and I had somehow missed out on ever finding my person.

Then there came the "I'm done with this" phase. When three years of singleness went by with no lasting relationships, I grew completely worn-out by the "gift" of singleness I had been given. I felt like my life did not matter. Everyone else seemed to be in relationships—friends, family, people on TV, and that couple obnoxiously making out at the park. Had I missed the sign-up sheet for the "relationship" life milestone that everyone else had filled out?

I wondered, *Why did God give me hopes and dreams of marriage only to not fulfill them? I thought God loved me, so why is He letting me be alone, growing hopeless and broken?* I begged and pleaded with God to stop my singleness, and He kept answering no. I did not understand that no. I absolutely hated that no, and I grew increasingly frustrated, angry, and heartbroken.

Do you relate to my struggle at all? Maybe you have never dated, maybe you just went through a breakup, or maybe you are widowed or divorced. No matter how you got to this place, being single can be completely exhausting, especially when you never wanted to be here in the first place.

Have you asked God to change your relationship status and gotten a no? Maybe you bitterly laugh at the thought of asking God because you know it will not change anything. You are not alone. We have suffered through this dilemma together.

And you know what? We are not alone in our struggle. There is also another very important person to whom God gave that smack-in-the-face answer, and His story gives me hope when God continuously tells me no. It might surprise you to learn who that person is. He is our very first bachelor. The one. The only. Jesus Christ.

The Bachelor: JESUS CHRIST

OCCUPATION: Carpenter/Savior
HOMETOWN: Nazareth
TATTOOS: Nope
PIERCINGS: Hands, feet, and side
TALENTS: Turning water into wine, raising people from the dead, *actually* being perfect

God told Jesus no.

That doesn't exactly match the heading of the story that was explained to me in Sunday school. The coloring sheet had a much less edgy title: "The Garden of Gethsemane." But that is the fateful place where Jesus (just like me, over and over) received His no from God.

Jesus went to the garden of Gethsemane with His disciples the night before He was crucified. As Jesus was walking through the garden with Peter, James, and John, He became deeply distressed, telling His disciples, "My soul is overwhelmed with sorrow to the point of death. Stay here and keep watch with me" (Matt. 26:38).

Let's pause the story right here.

Have you ever woken up in the morning and felt your heart sink as you realize what day it is? The day you take the test, give the presentation, get the results from the doctor, or have that difficult conversation you have been avoiding.

Every single morning of college finals felt that way for me. The days spent studying and preparing did not matter at all. When that alarm clock went off, I felt that getting out of bed to face the day was the equivalent of lining up to have an old-fashioned pistol duel. Anxiety flowed through me as each second brought me closer to the impending doom of finals.

Now imagine waking up in the morning, knowing your day would bring betrayal by one of your closest friends, abandonment from the rest, public mocking, gruesome torture, rejection by the people you love, punishment for all the sins of the world, and then death in one of the most excruciating ways possible. Jesus knew all that unfathomable misery would come to pass—the rejection, the pain, the loneliness, and the suffering. All those tragedies are the "sorrow to the point of death" He was describing.

As Jesus was thinking about what the near future would bring, He continued to walk in the garden alone. After He went a stone's throw away from Peter, James, and John, He fell in sorrow with His face to the ground. He said, "Father, if you are willing, take this cup from me; yet not my will, but yours be done" (Luke 22:42).

When Jesus said "cup," He was referring to all the terrible things that were going to happen to Him over the next day. Jesus was saying, "God, if there is another way, let it happen that way, but if not, I will face My future."

Jesus prayed this three times, and Luke writes, "Being in anguish, he prayed more earnestly, and his sweat was like drops of blood falling to the ground" (v. 44).

I have prayed for God to end my singleness, but I have never experienced "sweat like drops of blood" while praying. Crying and anger? You bet. But never have I come close to the intensity that Jesus had in His prayer in the garden of Gethsemane.

He prayed one of the most passionate and heartfelt prayers to God. But as we know (spoiler alert), there was not another way for Him to pay for the sins of the world. God said no to removing the loneliness, the sorrow, and the agony that was coming for His Son.

Does this make you relate to Jesus a little more? Jesus knew how a no felt, but He was facing a fate far worse than singleness (even though I know that can be pretty bad). The no Jesus received meant betrayal (yes, that is applicable to dating), rejection (yes, that is also applicable to dating), physical and emotional torture (yes, that can also be applicable to dating), the wrath of God (Jesus wins the pity party here), and death (if you are alive and reading this, then Jesus wins here too).

But the no Jesus received, and the path He took over the next twenty-four hours, meant He would face the worst possible circumstances willingly, because He knew that you would be born two thousand years later. Yes, you. And Jesus knew this path was worth it because He wanted to save you. The no was part of a much bigger and beautiful plan for *you*.

Jesus knows exactly what your loneliness, your sorrow, your heartbreak, and your rejection feel like. Spend a few minutes thinking about everything that happened from the garden of Gethsemane to Jesus's death. How Jesus went alone to be tortured, mocked, jeered at by crowds of people who hated Him, and killed with people watching in satisfaction at His death. And it did not end there. Jesus is still being rejected by billions of people every single day who do not want to believe what He did for them. His heart is full of love for these people, and they reject Him.

Jesus knows what it is like to be in life circumstances that seem completely overwhelming and depressing. He has felt all our emotions at a depth so much greater than we will ever know. But He faced it all because He loves you, and that is the most important piece of information. It's the key that has started to change my experience with singleness and can change yours as well. The key is not only understanding that Jesus knows what you are going through but understanding your identity in Him.

IDENTITY QUIZ

If I asked you to tell me five things about yourself, what would you say? What makes you, you?

1. _____

2. _____

3. _____

4. _____

5. _____

Unfortunately (or fortunately?), this book is not Tom Riddle's diary, so I cannot directly respond to you through these pages. However, I am going to walk alongside you as you learn to understand your identity. Not having a magical book just means that you will have to do more of the thinking rather than let the book think for you, which is probably better in the long-term anyway. (See diary outcome in *Harry Potter and the Chamber of Secrets*.)

Now, will you share what is on your identity list? What differentiates you from the other seven billion people in this world? Is it what you study or what you do for work? Is it your hobbies, special talents, accomplishments, or unique experiences? Is it personality traits or habits that define you?

Those identity pieces can all be positive things in life—and I hope your identity consists of positive things—but I know that they can also be very negative things. Maybe you were bullied as you grew up or given a label like "uncool," "unathletic," "underachieving," "ugly," or something else. Are those the words you have written on your list—are they informing the way you see yourself?

If you are honest, is "single" a key piece of your identity right now? Perhaps you did not write it down because you were afraid that someone would pick up this book and see what you wrote, but is how you see yourself at this present moment largely focused on your relationship status? You are self-conscious when you go places alone, you want to cringe when you see couples showing affection for each other, and so on.

When you look at your list and reflect on how you see yourself, does it answer the question, "Why do I matter?" Or does it answer, "Why don't I matter?"

Now that you have thought about your list, I will share mine with you. Throughout my life, I have answered this question of "Who am I?" many different ways. When I was young, I thought, *I am a Schermerhorn.* That did not just mean I had a last name with far too many letters; it meant that I belonged to a family I was proud to be a part of, and I wanted to act in accordance with that feeling. As I grew older, my identity became defined as I compared myself with others. I would label myself with things like "the smart one" or "the hard worker," and then I eventually added items like my grades, my friends, my athletic ability, my college, my degree, and my job to my list of identity markers.

We are such emotionally fragile human beings. We come into this world with an empty list, and we hunt and search for our identities—our sense of value and purpose on earth. We feel lost not knowing who we are and why we matter. When we find something we are good at—something that makes us stand out from those around us—we drench ourselves in it, making it our identity, simply because we are better at it than our peers. Yet after a lifetime of searching and trying to give ourselves value using our families, our careers, and our hobbies, we still end up feeling empty.

The problem with that approach is that your list can be completely wiped clean in a matter of seconds, and then what are you left with? Who are you, why do you matter, and how are you supposed to live your life? When I was in college, I allowed my list to become the core of who I was. I derived my meaning from my list, and my list defined why I thought I was important. My culmination of life experiences led me to base my identity in these things:

1. My abilities
2. My family
3. My relationship
4. My intelligence

I was a thriving (well, more like a struggling) engineering student. I prided myself in the fact that I was a hard worker, and even if I was surrounded by people smarter than me (which was always true), I could work extremely hard to get on the same level as them. I had a fantastic family that supported me. I was also engaged to be married and happily planning a wedding. I felt like the world was mine. My dreams were coming true, and I was very excited as I would soon add "wife" to my list of labels, as well as my future job title after graduation.

Then a series of bad events happened in a very short period of time. First, I was diagnosed with a rare combination of eye diseases that made me lose my vision in one eye. Up until that point, I felt somewhat invincible. I assumed my own abilities could get me through anything that I faced. But then I was forced to realize that some things were out of my control. In fact, if I was honest with myself, very few things were in my control—I could not even make my eye work correctly. I could not control my own body, so what could I really control in my life? The first strike came in my identity list.

1. ~~My abilities~~

Then, after battling many different health issues, my grandfather passed away. Months later, my mother had a cancer scare. These things made me realize that the family I prided myself in could be taken away from me in an instant. A second item got taken off the list.

2. ~~My family~~

During this same time, as you now know, my relationship went to smithereens as I called off a wedding and was thrown into singleness. I was heartbroken and alone. My third item was gone.

3. ~~My relationship~~

When all this was happening, I became extremely anxious and depressed. I would have panic attacks throughout the day and nightmares that would cause me to wake up and puke. It was war for me to get through each day, let alone each hour or minute sometimes. With these sorrows weighing me down, the grades and school achievements I used to care so much about began to slip away from me.

4. ~~My intelligence~~

Within weeks, each item on my list was made irrelevant, leaving me completely broken. There I was, realizing I had no control over my health, my family's lives, my relationships, or even my own talents. The foundations of everything that once defined me became unstable. I had no idea who I was or what I should do with my life now that I realized all the core pieces of my identity were able to change in an instant.

This was the hardest time in my life. I was a Christian and knew God loved me and was there for me, but honestly, that just led me to many prayers, with me begging Him to take me to heaven because I could not see any purpose left for me on earth. I did not feel like there was any meaning left in who I was or what my identity was. I felt better descriptors of my identity would be "broken," "failure," and "alone."

Take a look at your list again and start going through each line. What if you lost those pieces of your identity? What if you lost one of your talents or one of the other things that defines you? What if you lost them all? Maybe you already feel broken because there is something on your list that you wish were different. Is singleness so overpowering in your mind that it is ruling who you are and how you see yourself? Is it making you think you are not as important as other people?

Putting our identity in things that are beyond our control sets us up for failure, and I am a prime example of how terribly it plays out. Enjoying the blessings God has given us—our talents, people, experiences, and possessions—is wonderful. But if we see ourselves as a reflection of those flimsy things, our identity can easily disappear, then it is only a matter of time before we will have an identity crisis, because without them, who are we?

I found out how catastrophic it was to put my identity in the talents God had given me, the people He created, and the experiences He had given me. I was wrong to base my identity in the positive things, and I was wrong to base my identity in the negative things.

What I have learned is this: I felt my life was broken when my identity list was irrelevant. I tried to fill my list of who I was with so many reasons why I mattered. When those were gone, it seemed like they were only replaced by negative things. In reality, there is only one thing that should be written on my identity list.

LOVED BY GOD

I am not my successes. I am not my failures. I am not the positive things that people think of me, and I am not the negative things that people think about me. I am not a failed relationship, a crushed dream, or a broken heart. I am loved by God, and His love does not depend on my successes or failures. It is completely independent of my circumstances and can never be taken from me.

I am nothing more or nothing less than loved by God—the One who made the universe and loved me so much that He died for me because He thought to Himself, *You know what would make eternity so much better? Being able to spend it with Hannah.*

I am "loved by God."

A God who knows me better than anyone else, even myself. He knows everything that has ever happened to me and every thought that has ever crossed my mind. He understands exactly what I am going through. He has lived on earth; been betrayed and abandoned by His closest friends; faced loneliness, sorrow, and pain; and is still rejected by billions of people He cares about every single day. He knows what I am going through, He loves me through it all, and He is with me in every single breath of life.

An eternity of perfect love is ahead of me. What else could I need? What else could I want?

John, one of the biblical authors who wrote the book of—can you guess it?—John, had the chance to write a description of himself in Scripture. He had a blank slate to write what he would be known for. He could have written "John, the best-looking disciple" or "John, the most successful disciple" or "John, the disciple with the best dance moves," but what did he write about his identity? John 13:23 says, "the disciple whom Jesus loved."

I used to laugh at this sentence, thinking it sounded like bragging: "Oh, I'm the disciple Jesus loves. Not Peter, not James, but I, John, am the one He loves." I was very wrong with that interpretation.

John had the chance to say anything he wanted about himself—to tell future generations who he was—and he shared his entire identity in one sentence: "the disciple whom Jesus loved."

What a powerful statement!

I know that being single is hard. People are constantly putting you into the single category. Even when you fill out taxes, you have to tell the government you are single. Do not be consumed by the identity that the world has assigned to you. You are not your relationship status. You are loved by Jesus, the One who has agape love for you that does not change based on what you do. He is the One who loved you before you were born. The One who takes every step with you. The One whose heart breaks with yours and who knows every thought and feeling that you experience.

The One who wants you forever.

You are loved by God, and nothing can ever change that.

Go back to your identity list. How do you feel about surrendering your list to God? Pray about it. It is not easy to give up control of your identity list, but it is the first wonderful step you can take on our journey together. Can you give your relationship status, your hopes, your dreams, your successes and failures to God and then see yourself for who you really are?

"Loved by God."

DIVING DEEPER

1. As a child, what hopes and dreams did you have for your future?
2. What is your "story of singleness"?
3. What are the most difficult emotions you feel as a single person? Can you think of examples when Jesus had these same emotions?

4. Why is it hard to let go of the things that form your identity?

5. What would your life look like if being loved by God was your only identifier?

6. If your full identity rests in God, how does your relationship status affect you?

7. What other ways does God describe you? Look at John 1:12, John 15:15, and Ephesians 2:10 for some hints.

8. If you were to receive a letter from God telling you how He feels about you, what would it say? Try writing it down: "Dear [insert name]." Do not think too hard about it. Just start by writing what you would tell yourself if you were God and see what happens.

2

loneliness

SOMETIMES THE ONLY THING I want is a hug. Not a quick goodbye hug from a friend or an awkward meeting-someone-for-the-first-time hug, but a deeply encompassing and affectionate hug. The type of hug that assures me someone is with me to help me through my emotional and physical trials. The type of hug that gives me relief that a person is there to support me when I cannot stand on my own. The type of hug that signifies the closeness of sharing life with another human being who cares deeply about my soul.

But guess what? As much as I long for that type of hug, someone is not going to magically appear out of thin air and be able to make me feel loved and cherished with a hug. (In that circumstance, I would be too frightened to give that person a hug anyway.) I am alone, I have no one to hug, and wearing a "Free Hugs" T-shirt to get hugs from strangers is not going to satisfy the lonely ache in my heart.

In reality a hug is not *exactly* what I need. A hug symbolizes all the things I feel are lacking in my life that make me lonely. I long for someone who is physically close with me, emotionally understands me, is there to help me in trials, and genuinely cares about the person I am. So as much as I think a hug is what I want, what I actually need is a type of Spackle to fill the hole in my heart created by all of loneliness's wants and desires.

It is difficult to choose the hardest part of being single, but I think loneliness is one of the top contenders. Loneliness is an overpowering emotion that creeps into our lives in many unpredictable ways. It is easy for me to expect loneliness in the difficult times: when I get sick in the middle of the night with no one to help me and think, *How long will it take for someone to find my body if I die here alone? Days? Weeks? Months?* Or when I receive devastating news about myself or someone close to my heart. I have to process and face the hardship all alone. In the middle of the night, there is no one to cry to, to reassure me, or to gently remind me of God's love.

Loneliness affects not only the hardships but it can sneakily sting during the "joys" of life as well. During holidays, I am bombarded with social media posts of cute couples celebrating together paired with questions from my relatives wondering why I did not bring a "special someone" to the family gathering. When I go to the umpteenth wedding or baby celebration, it is hard to repress the selfish monster that asks, "Why did these people get this and not me?" and not to think, "Well, if I go, maybe I will meet someone I can date there."

One of the things that has shocked me the most about loneliness is how lonely the people I am close to can make me feel. If I ask someone for help and they fall through because of kids, a spouse, or some other reason, I feel like I am insignificant and a burden to other people. The messages from those experiences ring in my head that I will never be important enough. Something or someone will always trump me, and I can rely only on myself. It is hard to accept that, at most, I am the second priority to everyone.

Other times friends who have "achieved" more in life—by successfully attaining a significant other—will leave me out because they kindly do not want me to feel awkward being a third, fifth, or some other odd-numbered wheel. If they bypass the odd-wheel rule and I am graciously invited, the conversation typically centers on children and family—which is great—but I get the impression that I have the life of a pariah compared with all the families. If the conversation does turn to my life, most of those questions relate to dating in order to see when I can graduate to talking about my own family and children. If you are questioning whether you are in the situation I am describing, you simply need to wait for the key phrase, "I could not even imagine what it would be like to date anymore," and you'll know you are experiencing it with me!

MASKING YOUR LONELINESS

How has loneliness affected you in your singleness? Maybe, like me, you have experienced it in every corner of your life, from being home with no one to feeling alone in groups of people who do not understand you. Maybe loneliness has led you to wear a mask to cover your true feelings. You would love to honestly share with friends and family how you feel about your life, but when you begin to share your pain, people do not know what to say and quickly look for an exit from the conversation. They struggle to relate to what you are going through, so you stop sharing your daily highs and lows. You do not want to be a drain or burden on other peoples' lives, so instead, you pretend to be excited and talk about dating and act bubbly about your lack of a significant other. It is exhausting to project a fake, happy life. It seems easier than showing people the true pain within, but masking your true feelings only makes you feel more alone.

I wonder why God lets us experience a depth of loneliness that can feel like being lost at night with nothing to help us find our way. I wonder why God gave Eve to Adam by making her out of Adam's rib but will not even place a cute guy in the coffee shop that I frequent so we can magically fall in love.

How are we supposed to deal with the overwhelming emotion of loneliness in our single lives? How are we supposed to go through the ebb and flow of life alone? If you are struggling to understand how to satisfy your loneliness, you can learn from a man who was destined for a life without a partner and learned to overcome his loneliness.

There is a famous Bible passage that is put on cards, coffee mugs, and T-shirts that comes from this man's life: "'For I know the plans I have for you,' declares the LORD, 'plans to prosper you and not to harm you, plans to give you hope and a future'" (Jer. 29:11).

I never knew all the insane circumstances that led up to this encouraging Bible verse. This man lived one of the loneliest lives I have ever heard of, but the way he dealt with it and overcame the obstacles in his way has been an incredible example and hope for me. His life gives me confidence that I can follow his path to radiate the truth that I am never alone. Are you ready to journey with me to a place where we will no longer be overwhelmed with loneliness? If so, let's take a look at our next bachelor: Jeremiah.

The Bachelor:
JEREMIAH

OCCUPATION: Prophet

HOMETOWN: Anathoth

TALENTS: Perseverance, prophesying the future, having God's protection

What would be worse: being trapped on a deserted island for four years with a volleyball as your only companion or being surrounded by people—including friends and family—who despise you and look for every opportunity to kill you? I think the second one is worse, and our bachelor actually survived it.

The story of Jeremiah is found in the Old Testament. He lived in the kingdom of Judah, in a time when the Judeans had turned their hearts very far from God. What exactly were they doing that was so bad?

- Committing adultery and crowding the houses of prostitutes (5:7)
- "Neighing" for the wives of others (5:8)
- Committing evil deeds that had no limit (5:28)
- Prophesying lies to an audience who loved it (5:31)
- Stealing, murdering, and committing perjury, then coming before God in His house and saying, "'We are safe'— safe to do all these detestable things" (7:9-10)
- Setting up idols in the house of the Lord and burning their children in the fire (7:30-31)
- Worshiping multiple gods and burning incense to Baal (11:13)

Judah had become such a horrible place that God actually *commanded* Jeremiah to be single so that his children would not have to face the terrors that were coming as a result of the Judeans' sins. Can you imagine God commanding you to stay single? At least Jeremiah did not have to deal with dating apps.

In this kingdom full of people defying God, Jeremiah was not called to get a job at the nearby horse cart factory and quietly let his light shine to unbelieving coworkers as he designed innovative horse carts and waited for the occasional conversation to come up where he could give his opinion on child burning and his take on putting our hope in God. Jeremiah's life's work was to prophesy to the Judeans, to be loud in his message and defy their normal ways of thinking, to tell them that their actions were sinful and that God was going to destroy them if they did not repent. God told Jeremiah "to stand against the whole land—against the kings of Judah, its officials, its priests and the people of the land" (1:18). Jeremiah had to go knock on his neighbor Jedidiah's door and say, "Hey, you know how you visit prostitutes every night? That's wrong, and if you do not repent, God is going to allow Judea to be destroyed." And when people dressed up and went out at night, flocking to offer sacrifices to their false gods, Jeremiah was called to grab a megaphone and proclaim, "God is going to destroy Judea if you do not stop doing this!"

As you can guess, the Judeans began to loathe Jeremiah because of these negative messages. Instead of giving up their evil ways, they mocked and insulted Jeremiah. They did not keep their abuse to only emotional jabs; they hated him so much that they physically hurt him and plotted his murder. Here are two examples of Jeremiah's treatment—from the religious leaders! This would have been like Jeremiah walking into church to tell God's truth and receiving these reactions:

> When the priest Pashhur son of Immer, the official in charge of the temple of the Lord, heard Jeremiah prophesying these things, he had Jeremiah the prophet beaten and put in the stocks at the Upper Gate of Benjamin at the Lord's temple. (20:1-2)

> The priests, the prophets and all the people heard Jeremiah speak these words in the house of the Lord. But as soon as Jeremiah finished telling all the people everything the Lord had commanded him to say, the priests, the prophets and all the people seized him and said, "You must die!" (26:7-8)

Even the people of Jeremiah's own hometown—including his family—wanted to kill him. They said:

Let us destroy the tree and its fruit;
> let us cut him off from the land of the living,
> that his name be remembered no more. (11:19)

Despite everyone despising him, Jeremiah persisted in his message, day after day, warning the Judeans to repent. As a result, he continued to face even more terrible consequences of the Judeans' rejection: "Jeremiah was put into a vaulted cell in a dungeon, where he remained a long time" (37:16).

After family, prophets, priests, and the people of the land tried to kill him, he was placed in solitary confinement. Then yet another form of punishment was put upon him.

So they took Jeremiah and put him into the cistern of Malkijah, the king's son, which was in the courtyard of the guard. They lowered Jeremiah by ropes into the cistern; it had no water in it, only mud, and Jeremiah sank down into the mud. (38:6)

Which of the situations Jeremiah faced was the loneliest? His family trying to kill him? His friends? Being in solitary confinement and reflecting on the fact that everyone wanted him dead? Being thrown into a pit of mud to die of starvation while slowly sinking down into the muck? The worst part of all these situations is that every one of these things was done by the people he cared about and was trying to help.

When I consider the depth of loneliness that Jeremiah must have faced throughout his life, it's hard to throw a pity party for myself. How did Jeremiah get through his family trying to kill him? I can barely get through a wedding without succumbing to my lonely feelings. Jeremiah persisted through everything despite the life he was leading. He prophesied for nearly forty years until Nebuchadnezzar, the king of the Babylonians, destroyed Jerusalem and the temple in 586 BC. How did Jeremiah get up each morning and face his incredibly lonely life?

THE CURE FOR LONELINESS

Jeremiah brought his messy feelings and emotions to God. He did not attempt to hide them even though those emotions were negative, crushing, and raw. Jeremiah did not put up a wall in his mind so that he could ignore how difficult and depressing his life had become. He did not spend all his free moments binge-watching his favorite TV show so he would not have to process the fact that people were trying to kill him. And he did not walk around with music blasting in his ears to drown out the people yelling insults at him. Jeremiah fully acknowledged the reality of his difficult circumstances and brought his raw, hurt, and unfiltered emotions to God.

Throughout the book of Jeremiah, insightful dialogue between Jeremiah and God is recorded for us. It gives us many beautiful examples of Jeremiah being honest with God about his pain, and God reassuring Jeremiah in turn. I will show you a couple of examples of what this looks like. In chapter 15, Jeremiah begins speaking with God by lamenting that he was ever born: "Alas, my mother, that you gave me birth, a man with whom the whole land strives and contends! I have never lent nor borrowed, yet everyone curses me" (v. 10).

Jeremiah continues his conversation with God, being bold enough to directly tell God that his hardships are a result of following Him:

> Think of how I suffer reproach for your sake.
> When your words came, I ate them;
>   they were my joy and my heart's delight,
> for I bear your name,
>   LORD God Almighty.
> I never sat in the company of revelers,
>   never made merry with them;
> I sat alone because your hand was on me
>   and you had filled me with indignation.

Why is my pain unending
and my wound grievous and incurable? (vv. 15–18)

Have you ever been that honest with God? Have you ever even been that honest with yourself? I often feel negative emotions, but the moment I start feeling bad, I try to get rid of them as quickly as possible. When I feel frustration, anger, and sorrow, I do not take the time to lay each out and unpack them to see where they come from and what is truly going on in my mind. After a frustrating day at the office or at school, I would rather go home and binge-watch a show on Netflix while drinking a glass of wine so I don't have to process the stress I am feeling. When I am bored or lonely, I scroll through other people's social media updates to distract myself from paying attention to my own life. Even when I cross paths with someone in the hallway at work, I would rather pull out my phone and pretend to be distracted than make awkward eye contact or conversation with that person. I hate feeling uncomfortable, and I do everything I can to avoid it.

We live in a world full of distractions, but those distractions can be dangerous when we use them to cover up our negative emotions and prevent ourselves from understanding them. How will things get better if we keep burying them? The beautiful truth—as shown by Jeremiah—is that God wants us to work through our pain, our loneliness, and our disappointments with Him. *There is nothing in our minds so bad that God cannot handle it.*

God can help us dig in to why we are feeling pain and work through it, and most importantly, He gives us the truth and comfort we need to deal with all the hardships and sorrows we experience. He will help us with every dark thought, even if we are too afraid to share those thoughts with others.

When Jeremiah mourned over his loneliness and suffering, God responded with His loving truth: "I will make you a wall to this people, a fortified wall of bronze; they will fight against you but will not overcome you, for *I am with you* to rescue and save you" (v. 20, emphasis added).

What a statement! As you can see, God did not back away from Jeremiah's pain. God did not dismiss Jeremiah's suffering. He gave Jeremiah full assurance that He was with him in everything and would save him. And He did! God saved Jeremiah from all the terrible circumstances where people tried to hurt and kill him, and God ultimately saved him to live in bliss in heaven forever.

In Jeremiah 20, we see another similar conversation. Jeremiah again laid his agonizing thoughts before God:

> You deceived me, Lord, and I was deceived;
>> you overpowered me and prevailed.
> I am ridiculed all day long;
>> everyone mocks me.
> Whenever I speak, I cry out
>> proclaiming violence and destruction.
> So the word of the Lord has brought me
>> insult and reproach all day long . . .
> All my friends
>> are waiting for me to slip, saying,
> "Perhaps he will be deceived;
>> then we will prevail over him
>> and take our revenge on him." (vv. 7–8, 10)

Jeremiah poured out his unfiltered feelings, including his sorrows and fears over everyone mocking, insulting, and plotting against him. He felt like he would end his days in shame. But once again, we see the assurance that God's truth brings. In the middle of his sorrows, Jeremiah did not need God to give him reassurance this time. Jeremiah had confidence in God and declared,

> But the Lord is with me like a mighty warrior;
>> so my persecutors will stumble and not prevail.

They will fail and be thoroughly disgraced;
> their dishonor will never be forgotten.
Lᴏʀᴅ Almighty, you who examine the righteous
> and probe the heart and mind,
let me see your vengeance on them,
> for to you I have committed my cause.

Sing to the Lᴏʀᴅ!
> Give praise to the Lᴏʀᴅ!
He rescues the life of the needy
> from the hands of the wicked. (vv. 11–13)

It is easy for Satan to get into our minds and make us believe lies like "you are alone," "you will always suffer," and "the pain will never end." But *when we lay our fears and emotions before God, God can ease our suffering with His truth.*

God did this for Jeremiah, and He will do it for you and me. Despite the terrible circumstances Jeremiah faced, there is confidence in his declaration. He had hope and peace that God was fighting for him in every aspect of his life. Look at how Jeremiah triumphed over his loneliness. Look at how he even went as far as to praise God despite such a difficult life!

OVERCOMING LONELINESS

So what about you and me? We face incredible loneliness and everything that goes with it—rejection, disappointment, fear, and so many other heartbreaking emotions—in singleness. If Jeremiah could praise God when people were trying to kill him, then do you think we can get to a point where we can praise God in our loneliness as well?

I understand if that attitude feels unrealistic. I understand if you're thinking, *You don't know what I'm going through. You don't know what I've been through. If you had any idea, you would know I can't praise God in this. It would be another fake mask to wear.* I have thought the same thoughts. But as I study Jeremiah and look at his example, I believe that there is a better way to live our lives than succumbing to our loneliness and pain. We can control these thoughts and triumph over them. We can acknowledge that the difficult feelings are there, but it is our choice whether we let them overtake our lives or give them to God and let Him fill us with joy and confidence. Jeremiah has shown us how to do this. Let's apply his example to our lives with five simple steps.

1. Identify Your Lonely Times

The first thing Jeremiah did was bring his true feelings before God. Our to-do list starts with the important step of creating some emotional space to be raw with God. This may look different for you and me, so you need to find the way that works best for you. It might be starting a prayer journal and writing out your feelings to God. It may be creating art that shows the negative emotions you are feeling and the circumstances that cause them. It may just be closing your eyes and talking to God through prayer.

Once you've picked a method, start a timer and spend just ten minutes identifying what events have made you feel the loneliest in your life or what has recently made you feel lonely.

If Jeremiah made a list, it might look like this:

EVENTS

The people in my hometown tried to kill me.

The prophets, priests, and Judeans tried to kill me.

I was placed in solitary confinement.

I was thrown in a cistern to die of starvation.

I can't really compete with those, but I have had my fair share of lonely moments.

EVENTS

My friends did not invite me to a party because I would be the only single person there.

I went to a wedding and saw another happy couple getting married, and it wasn't me.

I was in France in a crowd of people by myself and couldn't understand a word anyone was saying.

I watched *Pride and Prejudice* and saw that Elizabeth and Darcy have each other, but I have no one.

So now it's your turn. What events have made you feel lonely? Feel free to write down as many as you can think of.

EVENTS

2. Identify the Lies

Satan, being the evil trickster he is, likes to fuel our loneliness with fears and lies so we get so engulfed that it becomes difficult to swim out. Look at your list of lonely events and think about what fears and lies enter your mind and make you feel that way.

Let's take a look at the things that may have troubled Jeremiah.

EVENTS	FEARS/LIES
The people in my hometown tried to kill me.	I am alone and will be destroyed.
The prophets, priests, and Judeans tried to kill me.	I am in this fight alone.
I was placed in solitary confinement.	My life is horrible, and I am destined for bad things.
I was thrown in a cistern to die of starvation.	No one cares about me; everyone hates me.

The lies and fears that creep into my mind are:

EVENTS	FEARS/LIES
My friends did not invite me to a party because I would be the only single person there.	I am not important. I will not be good enough or valued until I am dating.
I went to a wedding and saw another happy couple getting married, and it wasn't me.	My future has nothing important or meaningful in it.
I was in France in a crowd of people by myself and couldn't understand a word anyone was saying.	No one understands me.
I watched *Pride and Prejudice* and saw that Elizabeth and Darcy have each other, but I have no one.	No one loves me.

It's your turn.

EVENTS	FEARS/LIES

loneliness

EVENTS	FEARS/LIES

3. Crush the Fears

Now comes the extremely important part. We need to crush the lies and fears that Satan gets us to believe. Spend some time with God, pray about your lonely events, fears, and lies, and then see what scriptural truths you can find.

Again, let's start with Jeremiah's list:

EVENTS	FEARS/LIES	SCRIPTURAL TRUTH
The people in my hometown tried to kill me.	I am alone and will be destroyed.	"I will make you a wall to this people, a fortified wall of bronze; they will fight against you but will not overcome you, for I am with you to rescue and save you." (15:20)
The prophets, priests, and Judeans tried to kill me.	I am in this fight alone.	"But the LORD is with me like a mighty warrior." (20:11)
I was placed in solitary confinement.	My life is horrible, and I am destined for bad things.	"'For I know the plans I have for you,' declares the LORD, 'plans to prosper you and not to harm you, plans to give you hope and a future.'" (29:11)

45

EVENTS	FEARS/LIES	SCRIPTURAL TRUTH
I was thrown in a cistern to die of starvation.	No one cares about me; everyone hates me.	"I have loved you with an everlasting love; I have drawn you with unfailing kindness." (31:3)

Here are mine:

EVENTS	FEARS/LIES	SCRIPTURAL TRUTH
My friends did not invite me to a party because I would be the only single person there.	I am not important. I will not be good enough or valued until I am dating.	"The LORD your God is with you, the Mighty Warrior who saves. He will take great delight in you; in his love he will no longer rebuke you, but will rejoice over you with singing." (Zeph. 3:17)
I went to a wedding and saw another happy couple getting married, and it wasn't me.	My future has nothing important or meaningful in it.	"'For I know the plans I have for you,' declares the LORD, 'plans to prosper you and not to harm you, plans to give you hope and a future.'" (Jer. 29:11)
I was in France in a crowd of people by myself and couldn't understand a word anyone was saying.	No one understands me.	"Then they prayed, 'Lord, you know everyone's heart.'" (Acts 1:24)
I watched *Pride and Prejudice* and saw that Elizabeth and Darcy have each other, but I have no one.	No one loves me.	"For I am convinced that neither death nor life, neither angels nor demons, neither the present nor the future, nor any powers, neither height nor depth, nor anything else in all creation, will be able to separate us from the love of God that is in Christ Jesus our Lord." (Rom. 8:38–39)

What are yours? You don't need to be a Bible guru to find scriptural truths. All you need to do is Google some keywords from your lies along with words like *passages* or *Bible*, and you should be directed to websites full of passages that show you the truth.

EVENTS	FEARS/LIES	SCRIPTURAL TRUTH

4. Pray

After you finish this chart, spend some time praying to God about what you've discovered. For example, I would pray,

God, I am really upset that my friends didn't invite me to the party this weekend. I am so sick of being left out because I am not dating anyone. I feel like my value is in my relationship status and that I am not important or will not be valued until I am dating. You tell me that You are with me, You love me, and You even rejoice over me just as I am. Thank You for giving me so much value and caring about me so much.

5. Make It Your Own!

I am an engineer, so I have created a very formulaic method to go about curing loneliness. In theory, the more you take these steps, the more practice your brain will get, and then, when a lonely situation comes up, your brain will automatically remind you of the scriptural truth you need in that moment, and you won't even have to dissect your loneliness to understand it.

I encourage you to make this process your own. For example, sometimes I add a column called "I am not Jeremiah." (I apologize if that is, in fact, your name and that makes this a little more complicated.) What does the "I am not Jeremiah" column mean? It is where I think about how blessed I am to live in the world, community, and time that God has placed me in. Sometimes I am so focused on what I think is wrong that I forget how blessed I am. Hence the "I am not Jeremiah" column. Take a look:

EVENTS	FEARS/LIES	SCRIPTURAL TRUTH	I AM NOT JEREMIAH
My friends did not invite me to a party because I would be the only single person there.	I am not important. I will not be good enough or valued until I am dating.	"The LORD your God is with you, the Mighty Warrior who saves. He will take great delight in you; in his love he will no longer rebuke you, but will rejoice over you with singing." (Zeph. 3:17)	I have so many amazing friends around me that I can hang out with.
I went to a wedding and saw another happy couple getting married, and it wasn't me.	My future has nothing important or meaningful in it.	"'For I know the plans I have for you,' declares the LORD, 'plans to prosper you and not to harm you, to give you hope and a future.'" (Jer. 29:11)	I was invited to a wedding because people care about me and wanted me there.

EVENTS	FEARS/LIES	SCRIPTURAL TRUTH	I AM NOT JEREMIAH
I was in France in a crowd of people by myself and couldn't understand a word anyone was saying.	No one understands me.	"Then they prayed, 'Lord, you know everyone's heart.'" (Acts 1:24)	I was in France!
I watched *Pride and Prejudice* and saw that Elizabeth and Darcy have each other, but I have no one.	No one loves me.	"For I am convinced that neither death nor life, neither angels nor demons, neither the present nor the future, nor any powers, neither height nor depth, nor anything else in all creation, will be able to separate us from the love of God that is in Christ Jesus our Lord." (Rom. 8:38–39)	British literature is very entertaining! I am glad God had Jane Austen live before me so I can enjoy her writing.

GOD IS ALWAYS HERE

Now, hopefully these steps have helped you hit the things that make you feel lonely square in the face, but the underlying lie Satan is trying to tell us when it comes to loneliness is that we truly are alone. Seems pretty obvious, right? Even so, I want us to take a little more time to digest this one. This was on my chart, I'm sure it would have been on Jeremiah's, and it may be on yours as well.

There are many scriptural truths that assure us of the opposite of this lie, like Matthew 28:20, in which God says, "Surely I am with you always, to the very end of the age." But sometimes it is hard to really believe that truth. It feels more like a fairy tale made for a world we do not live in.

49

I have a theory about some of the things that will happen to us when we go to heaven. This is not in the Bible; this is simply me imagining what it will be like. When we die and go to heaven, I feel like we will sit in a theater with God and eat popcorn as we watch the story of our lives. We all have our own version of our life story in our minds where there are lots of questions and gaps. Why did we have to suffer through that? Why did we not get that opportunity? Why did God let that happen to our family? We face so many things that hurt us, break our hearts, and shatter our lives, and we wonder, *Why did this happen to me? Did You even care that I was going through that, God?*

But when we sit in that theater with God, He is going to show us the real story of our lives. God will show us how He was with us in every single moment, in every step we took, and in every breath, guiding us, comforting us, and directing us toward ultimate happiness with Him in heaven. He'll tell us, "I was there when your heart broke, I was there when you felt alone, I was there when you thought you could not overcome, and I was there when you hated yourself." He will show us how all these things were part of His master plan—how the heartbreak led us to something else, how we were alone in order to avoid some terrible event, how He strengthened us when we thought we couldn't overcome, how He forgave us when we hated ourselves. He will say, "There was not a time when I left you, and there will never be a time when you are alone." And we will finally understand how truly encompassing God's love and presence is.

Now imagine watching that movie from God's perspective right now. Would it change how you live? Do you think it would be almost impossible to feel lonely when you *know* you have Him with you in every single moment? Remember the truth: *You are never alone!*

God is always right beside you. He knows how you feel, He knows who you are better than anyone else, and He will never leave you.

DIVING
DEEPER

1. Consider some historical, biblical, and modern-day examples of lonely people. What kept them lonely or allowed them to thrive in their circumstances?

2. When were you the loneliest in your whole life? What were the circumstances?

3. What lies and fears have accompanied your loneliness?

4. Think of a time you felt the least lonely. What were the circumstances?

5. What Bible passage gives you the most comfort when you feel lonely?

6. If you haven't already, go through the five steps to crush your loneliness.

7. Why is it difficult to believe God is always with you?

8. How does truly believing that God is with you change the way you live your life?

9. Apply Deuteronomy 31:6, Isaiah 41:10, Isaiah 43:1–7, and Romans 8:31–39 to your life.

3

waiting

ONE COLD WISCONSIN WINTER DAY, I was walking through the hallways of my college when something very strange happened. Suddenly, my world turned into a frightening, fictional universe where people's heads shrunk to be really tiny, and the rest of their bodies became overinflated balloons.

I blinked and rubbed my eyes, thinking, *This is what you get for doing so much homework.* But as I tried to blink away the sight, everyone's bodies remained horrifyingly disproportional. Nothing I did would change it. *Am I dreaming? Am I hallucinating?* I panicked. This was real life.

I tried to wipe the horror off my face as people looked at me. I took a deep breath. Then I had another idea. I closed my left eye and felt the rushing sensation of relief as people's bodies returned to their normal proportions. I did the same with my right eye, and all of a sudden it looked like I had a fun house mirror filter over my vision that turned everyone back into balloons.

The panic I had been ignoring started screaming inside again. Naturally, I did the most logical thing: I googled my problem. The internet told me that I was most likely going to die from some horrible disease that was altering my vision. Then my anxiety soared so high I decided the best course of action was to sleep off my problem. Maybe while I was sleeping, my eyeball would decide it would want to function as a normal eyeball once again.

My eyeball did not listen. I woke up with the same fun house mirror vision in my left eye. I made doctor's appointments, had lots of tests done, and eventually found myself sitting in the waiting room of an eye clinic.

The seconds on the clock ticked by as I tried to stay calm, hoping my name would get called so I could leave the miserable waiting room. I was surprised other patients were not staring at me because I felt like my heart was pounding so fast and loud that everyone else could hear it drumming.

You see, my doctor had figured out that I had two eye diseases with much longer and more complicated names than "blindness" and "fun house mirror." One of those diseases had caused a blood vessel to grow straight through the middle of my eye so that I could no longer see. Thanks, eyeball.

All that led to me sitting in the waiting room, exploding with anxiety before my first treatment: a shot in my eye. If you are like any other normal human being I have told this story to, I know to spare you any more details about that procedure (that is, if you haven't already thrown this book down, saying, "Nope, I can't read more about this!").

Even without the gory details, I bet you can imagine all the emotions going through my head as I waited in the seemingly calm room, desperately hoping to be released from the mental torture so I could just get on with my life. Around me, the receptionist smiled and people were talking while I was sitting there in agony. I remember thinking, *Please, get me out of the waiting room!*

No matter how much time ticked by, all I could do was wait. If I ran out, I would never be healed, but I could also do nothing to make a nurse call my name any faster. I was completely trapped in the waiting.

I'M NEXT . . . AREN'T I?

As I think about that waiting room, it honestly is not the worst waiting room that I have felt confined to. The worst waiting room I have been in did not have a friendly staff and four walls with fascinating eyeball art. The "waiting room" that has destroyed me for a long time now is singleness.

After I broke off my engagement, a plethora of kind people came to me with encouraging stories of how they or one of their friends had also faced the tragedy of a broken engagement. After the horrible heartbreak, it took only a few months or even weeks for the people in these stories to meet their significant other and have a Hallmark-movie happily ever after. The well-meant encouragements always ended with something like, "See, God has even better plans for you than what you wanted, because that's how I met Greg, and we've been happily married for the last thirty years."

After a year of singleness passed and I began to date, those stories filled me with hope. I thought, *OK, God, I guess my ex wasn't the right one, but plot twist, now I am actually ready to meet an even better guy!*

Weeks turned into months that turned into years. I grew impatient in the singles' waiting room with my name never being called. Numerous people came into the room after me and all got called out before me. It felt so unfair. I sat through so many engagements, weddings, and questions about when I would be next. I tried to be happy for my friends, but I felt stuck in a life that I did not choose. Why couldn't I be like everyone else who was happily finding their significant others?

I tried everything to get out of the waiting room. I went on setups and blind dates, but all those dates gave me were comical stories to share with my friends. I went to places that the type of guy I would want to date would go—church, volunteer events, weddings, coffee shops, libraries, dance parties, Germany, anywhere!—but there was no one there for me. I pleaded with God to end my singleness, but He did not answer that prayer with a yes. I would meet promising guys only to find out—of course, after getting my hopes up—that they were not right for me. Eventually, my hope completely faded in having a happy ending. My patience ran out. I felt completely alone. I did not understand why this had to be the reality of my life when I had hoped for so much more.

If you are in this waiting room with me, I want to share an encouraging story that has helped me understand the answers to the questions "Why do I need to be stuck here when I hate it?" and "What could the point of this waiting room possibly be?" Let's take a look at the story of our next bachelor, Lazarus, to see what the answers to those questions might be.

The Bachelor:
LAZARUS

HOMETOWN: Bethany
FAMILY: Mary and Martha
TALENTS: Zombie impressions

There was a man named Lazarus who was trapped in a waiting room of sickness. His illness quickly pulled him close to death. Lazarus's sisters, Mary and Martha, could do nothing to help their brother, so they desperately reached out to the one person they knew could help: Jesus. Their message said, "Lord, the one you love is sick" (John 11:3).

If you received a text message right now that a person you love is sick—potentially on-the-verge-of-death sick—what would you do? I would probably run to my car, run back into my house and set out a weeks' worth of cat food, then run back to my car and speed to the hospital to see my loved one.

But look at Jesus's reaction (granted, He probably did not have a cat): "Now Jesus loved Martha and her sister and Lazarus. So when he heard that Lazarus was sick, he stayed where he was two more days" (vv. 5-6).

Get that? *Jesus loved them, so He chose to wait.*

Mary and Martha waited day after day for Jesus to show up. They were powerless to change the impending tragedy on their own. The minutes and hours passed with Lazarus only getting worse, but Jesus did not show up to end their suffering. After a few more days of waiting, Lazarus died. Four days after Lazarus was buried in a tomb, Jesus arrived.

Before we take a look at what Jesus did when He finally showed up, I'm going to spoil the end of this story for you: Jesus raised Lazarus from the dead (gasp!).

Now, if you were Jesus in this situation—on your way to visit Mary and Martha, knowing that you would miraculously raise their brother from the dead in a few moments—how would you approach them? I would stroll over with a huge smile on my face, thinking, *Oh, just wait and see what is coming, ladies, this is going to be good!*

Jesus knew the good that was coming, but take a look at His reaction:

> When Mary reached the place where Jesus was and saw him, she fell at his feet and said, "Lord, if you had been here, my brother would not have died."
>
> When Jesus saw her weeping, and the Jews who had come along with her also weeping, *he was deeply moved in spirit and troubled.* "Where have you laid him?" he asked.
>
> "Come and see, Lord," they replied.
>
> *Jesus wept.*
>
> Then the Jews said, "See how he loved him!" (vv. 32–36, emphasis added).

If you feel stuck in a waiting room in some aspect of your life, this part of the story should be a huge comfort. Jesus allowed Lazarus, Mary, Martha, and many others to go through suffering and extreme agony and sorrow. But as He did, Jesus was not simply eating popcorn and waiting for things to get better. He felt the pain they were feeling. He agonized and suffered with them. His heart broke with theirs.

The same is true for you. Jesus knows how your story will end, but He cries and suffers with you in your hurt. He feels your pain even though He knows everything will work out for you. You are not alone in your suffering. *God does not simply watch you go through pain; He experiences it with you.*

Jesus is right there crying with you. And you know what? Your happy ending will come just as it did for Lazarus:

> Jesus called in a loud voice, "Lazarus, come out!" The dead man came out, his hands and feet wrapped with strips of linen, and a cloth around his face.
>   Jesus said to them, "Take off the grave clothes and let him go." (vv. 43–44)

Imagine that scene from Mary and Martha's perspective! Imagine your dead brother being raised from the dead after all hope seemed lost. I have received news that my friends or family were now cancer-free after years of suffering, and that feels like the best news. Seeing your loved one raised from the dead is a level of joy I am not sure I will ever understand on this side of death.

The painful waiting room, the dark turn of dying, and the positive impact of being raised from the dead are all parts of Lazarus's story.

So, what is the point of it all? Jesus could have come in the beginning and saved everyone a whole lot of suffering by healing Lazarus right away. Why did He choose to let them wait?

Three times in this story, Jesus tells us exactly what God was doing (emphasis is mine).

1. When Jesus first received the news that Lazarus was sick, He said, "This sickness will not end in death. No, it is for God's glory so that *God's Son may be glorified through it*" (v. 4).
2. Then after Jesus waited, He knew that Lazarus had died. When He told His disciples the news, He told them He was glad He was not there to help "so that *you may believe*" (v. 15).
3. Before Jesus raised Lazarus from the dead, He stood in front of the tomb and prayed to God. He prayed for the benefit of those listening, so "that *they may believe* that you sent me" (v. 42).

Jesus could have gone and healed Lazarus right away, but instead He decided to wait. If He had gone immediately, the people would have seen a clear display of the compassion Jesus had for Lazarus and his family. Which sounds great, right?

However, God had bigger plans for the people in this story, and He does for you as well. Because Jesus loved them—and because He loves you—He decided to wait. In the waiting, God gave everyone something that was much greater than what they asked or hoped for. Instead of just healing Lazarus, Jesus showed He had even greater power and authority by raising him from the dead. This did not have implications for just Mary, Martha, and Lazarus. It led to many new followers. John 12 says,

> Meanwhile a large crowd of Jews found out that Jesus was there and came, not only because of him but also to see Lazarus, whom he had raised from the dead. So the chief priests made plans to kill Lazarus as well, *for on account of him many of the Jews were going over to Jesus and believing in him.* . . .

Now the crowd that was with him when he called Lazarus from the tomb and raised him from the dead continued to spread the word. Many people, because they had heard that he had performed this sign, went out to meet him. So the Pharisees said to one another, "See, this is getting us nowhere. Look how the whole world has gone after him!" (vv. 9–11, 17–20)

God keeps us in waiting rooms so that He can advance His glorious plans for our lives.

I know as I feel trapped in my waiting room of singleness, life can honestly feel empty and pointless. Friends are getting married or having kids, and it's like nothing is happening in my life. Hours and days blow away like dandelion seeds in the wind, barely seeming to make an impression in the moment. But when the time comes, look at the impact all those small, seemingly worthless seeds make (to the horror of people taking care of their lawn and to the delight of small children who can now give gifts to all their friends and family).

Do not lose hope. God is using every moment, every second of your life, to create a much bigger, more beautiful picture than you could ever imagine. *Our finite plans will always be outdone by God's infinite plans.*

He has more in store for us than we have ever hoped or asked for.

That sounds like a great concept, right? But what does that look like in practice? One day, in the waiting, God gave me a tiny glimpse into all the beautiful things He had been working on while I felt trapped in my unwanted circumstances.

SKELLIG ISLAND

Two facts about me: One, a few years ago, I went on a vacation to Ireland. Two, I am a huge *Star Wars* fan—like my friends and I broke numerous things with lightsabers growing up.

How do these two things go together? Thanks for asking. I'll tell you. There is a landmass called Skellig Island located off the west coast of Ireland. If you have seen any of episodes VII through IX of the *Star Wars* movies, you might recognize this green mountainous island as the home of the beehive huts and porgs.

After decades of trying to convince my parents to go to Europe, they finally agreed to join me on a trip to Ireland (miracles do happen!). We selected our dates to visit the gorgeous country, and after learning that Skellig Island was off the coast, I excitedly added it to our itinerary.

To prepare for Skellig Island, I found a video of a happy Irishman to guide me through everything the journey would entail. As I watched, the enthusiasm in my belly was rather quickly replaced with amplifying anxiety. I mentally started my list of every reason I should not do this trip.

Fear 1: Journey across the Deep, Dark Ocean

First, the trip required taking a tiny boat across the ocean to get to the island. If the weather was bad, the sea would be extremely rough. With bad weather, there was a high chance of either the trip getting canceled or the passengers getting terrible motion sickness (which I get). As the Irishman spoke, I pictured twenty-foot waves coming at my small, uncovered boat in the middle of the ocean. I would fall into the sea and face one of my greatest fears—the deep ocean where giant, dark, creepy animals live, and I would see them lurking toward me right before I died from lack of oxygen.

Fear 2: Getting Crushed between a Boat and Rocks

If we safely arrived at the island, the next step would be getting off the boat and onto land. For this step, the video showed a boat obnoxiously rocking back and forth in the sea. Passengers had to carefully synchronize their jump with the undulation of the waves, jumping at the right time from the boat onto the rocks of the island. Guides would be there to help, but if something went wrong, I could get crushed between the boat and the rocks.

Fear 3: Heights and Deadly Drop-Offs

After jumping and not getting crushed, I could bask in the gloriousness of the island, right? Wrong! To get to the top of the island, where the beehive huts are located, I would need to walk up four hundred stairs. These stairs are giant stones created by monks over one thousand years ago, and at that time, the monk builders failed to include a railing. That means that there were massive drop-offs on the side of the stairs, especially at the six-hundred-feet-high top. Also the path had sharp turns. If I missed a turn, I would walk right off a cliff and into the ocean. Did I mention I am afraid of heights?

Fear 4: Peeing My Pants on a Majestic Island

All these facts were difficult for me to hear, but the end of the video brought my biggest fear. This whole trip would take about six hours, and there would be no bathroom.

After watching the overview video, my parents graciously (and wisely) backed out of this excursion due to fear of heights and motion sickness. However, they were happy to work our vacation around Skellig Island and encouraged me to go if it was something I wanted to do. I contemplated looking up stats on dying or getting injured, then decided, *When else will I get this opportunity? I better do it.*

Skellig Island is a historical site of Ireland, meaning only a certain number of people are allowed to step foot on the island every year. Those spots are extremely difficult to obtain. I did my research and knew the exact minute that I had to go online to secure my spot. I was even extra-prepared: I had my mom ready at her computer to book the minute the slots opened. The seconds ticked past, and the minute finally came. Only there was a huge problem: excessive traffic on the website prevented both my mother and I from booking anything. After thirty minutes of trying, we finally got on the website, but every single spot was already taken.

I was disappointed but consoled myself by thinking, *Maybe the sea or height would have been too much for me. Perhaps this is God planning what is best for me.* But I couldn't completely let go of my dream of going to the island, so I desperately searched for alternate options. Unfortunately, I could find no remaining (legal) ways of getting to the island.

About a month later, as I was searching another website, the booking page for Skellig Island came up in my history as a suggested site. I decided to click the link to look at the beautiful island one more time. Suddenly my heart skipped a beat as I saw that one slot had opened up. And somehow, miraculously, it was during the time that I would be in Ireland. It was not the original day I planned on going—we would have to rearrange the trip to accommodate—but it was an opening! With a huge smile on my face and a heart full of giddiness, I immediately booked the last seat on the trip.

Ireland is known for many things, including Guinness, sheep, and rainy weather. Because the weather is typically stormy, I mentally acted like my Skellig Island excursion was not going to happen since it was very likely the weather would not cooperate. The night before the excursion came, my phone did not buzz with a notification that the trip was canceled (but it could still get canceled the day of). The early morning arrived, and my parents drove me to the dock as I tried to suppress my hope. As people gathered, I was finally given the news. The trip was on!

I hugged my parents goodbye and was nervous for the sea and the height, but guess what? My fears had absolutely no grounding. We sailed to the island on a beautiful day. It was magical—the sea was completely smooth, and dolphins were jumping in the wake of the boat. We saw puffins flying around, as well as some sea otters, and I got a bonus when my guide pointed out an island that was in a Harry Potter film. It was an unbelievably amazing journey! After the trip, the Irish locals even told me it was one of the best weather days they had ever seen.

Alighting from the boat was completely smooth because the water was completely calm.

The island was breathtaking. It felt like I had fallen into a fantasy world. Puffins were everywhere, waddling across the stairs into their burrows and flying like their bodies were too big for their wings. I journeyed up all the stairs very cautiously and was surprised at how little the height affected me. Just as I reached the beehive huts at the top of the island, the sun began to shine out from the clouds. I was even able to take off the numerous layers of coats I was wearing to protect me from the cold, wet Irish weather.

As the sun beamed, our guide told the history of Skellig Island. She explained how monks had traveled there thousands of years ago to get away from people and spend time with God. On the other peak of the island, monks would go out on a stone cliff and face the west (toward America). This was before they knew what was out there. They would go and pray to God, literally facing the unknown, and find their comfort and solitude in Him.

As I listened to this story, I happened to look at my phone and my heart skipped a beat. It was May 31. That might seem like a random day to you, but not for me. That was the date I was supposed to get married four years earlier. That was the date that every year since I had let myself sob over how my life had turned out and how unhappy I was about it. But this year, May 31 was one of the best days of my life.

I do not believe in coincidences. I felt like God had planned that perfect day to remind me of His love. As I looked out at the ocean with the sun shining down, I felt like God was saying, "I love you, and I have so much planned for you. Do you see how much I can change things in four years? See how much heartache you had and how you thought your future was being ruined? But, in fact, all those hardships have resulted in a life that is so much better for you than the life you planned for yourself. I'm going to keep doing that for you, Hannah. Trust Me in the trials and the hurts. Just like all your fears were for nothing on this trip, the same is true for your life. I'm guiding you to what is best for you, to a truly magical destination. Trust Me. I love you."

There is a plan. If my life had turned out the way I begged God to let it, I never would have had that beautiful day on the island (which, after a year of successful visual treatments, I could see with two functioning eyes) and I never would have experienced so much growth and beauty and depth in my relationship with God.

You may feel stuck in a waiting room of singleness, or you may feel like nothing is happening in your life, but God is working in every moment to weave things out beautifully for you, just like He did for Lazarus and just like He did for me. His plan may not align with yours, but I promise you it will be better for you than any plan you could have made for yourself.

DIVING DEEPER

1. In what areas of your life do you struggle to see God's plan?

2. What life events or milestones do you feel like you are missing out on?

3. What good has God caused to happen in your waiting?

4. Have you ever prayed for something and received something much greater than what you asked for?

5. What Bible passages give you reassurance that God has a plan for you?

6. Can you recall a Skellig Island moment in your life?

7. Lazarus was not the only single person trapped in a waiting room. For similar stories of how God's plan unfolds in waiting rooms, read:

- Mark 5—Demon-possessed man who lived in tombs and could not be bound
- John 5—A paralytic of thirty-eight years
- Luke 7:11–17—Widow whose only son had just died
- John 9—Man born blind

4

baggage

I AM ENVIOUS of my parents' and grandparents' dating experiences. Sending each other handwritten letters in the mail. Making phone calls from the one telephone on their dorm room floor. It all seems so simple. Today the fact that two humans can constantly be in communication—even if they are not physically next to each other—adds a whole new level of complexity to dating. When a new relationship is going well, the technology is a dear friend. You may be in a boring meeting or class when you have to repress a big smile or laugh as you read a text message from the person you are dating. You can have the emotional high that someone cares about the cinnamon roll production line you just created in the tiny oven you keep in your cube, how you took a picture of someone's background on a Zoom call and made it look like you were working from their house, or how you used boxes lying around your office to make a robot that is named after one of your coworkers.

But then there are the times in dating when technology is very cruel. Unfortunately, this is the side of technology that I am much more familiar with.

This fiend comes out when you send a text message to the person you like. After you reread your message ten times, decide it's fine, and breathe in nervously as you hit send, you try to put your phone in a place that says, "It's fine if I don't look at my phone for a while. I'm not waiting for anything *important* from it." But then you pick it up every minute, wondering if you missed the *ding* that announces the recipient has responded. After doing this for over an hour, you put your phone in a more "hidden" place, like under a blanket or in another room, hoping that if your phone is out of sight, you will forget about it. Ten minutes later, you somehow find yourself in that room with the phone in hand, staring at the screen that shows you have no new messages. You throw the phone down and decide you need a distraction as you remind yourself that it's not a big deal. You barely know this person, and all your happiness should not rest on them. But as the hours roll by, you start to wonder what that person is doing that they cannot take, at most, one minute to respond. Did they lose their phone? Is their phone not working? Is your phone not working? Are they fatally injured and in the hospital? Did they get abducted by aliens? Did they go for a run, drop their phone, and then watch as it got run over by a car?

As you consider all these possibilities, your ears—which suddenly have impeccable hearing—hear that glorious *ding* announcing a new message. You smile, roll your eyes at how ridiculous you felt five seconds ago, and pull up your phone with excitement. As you look at the screen, your energy instantly plummets as you see the message is not from the person you texted all those hours ago. It's just a text from your mom, asking how your meeting went. As more time passes with no response, you go into brooding mode, feeling disappointed, and you start telling yourself, *I don't need that person.* Or, *How did I let myself get excited about someone I barely know again?* Maybe they text you eventually or maybe you never hear from them. Either way, this all-too-common occurrence can leave you feeling unimportant, worthless, frustrated, and hopeless.

Has that ever happened to you? It has happened to me more times than I can count, and it is one of a bazillion frustrating experiences that have influenced how I feel today about dating.

UNPACKING THE BAGGAGE

How do your past relationship experiences affect your life today? If you have a desire to date, are you filled with hope and excitement for what the future may bring? Or are you more like me: completely exhausted by the thought of even trying to go on a date.

I used to live in the positive camp. It was a beautiful place with dreams of easily finding my person and falling in love. The men I would meet in the future would be interested in me and be kind, honest, and considerate. Maybe it would not work out with some of them, but that would not discourage me from finding my wonderful person. If you are there right now, I am jealous of you. I would love to stay in that place and be filled with hope for as long as possible. Unfortunately, my many years of bad dating experiences have slowly worn my high hopes completely down. Those situations have brought me to a point where I feel like I do not have the energy to send even one more text message to a prospective mate. Why try dating someone if it will only end in torturous disappointment? Maybe I have just become cynical, but modern dating can be incredibly exhausting and the rejection, crushed hope, and careless treatment from people you are trying to date can create some heavy baggage.

Has dating created any baggage for you? Maybe you have never dated and your self-esteem has plummeted as every person you have a crush on ignores you and dates someone else. Why can you never be the one? Maybe you are sick of wasting time going on dates, getting to like someone, then being devastated as you find out that your relationship will not last. Maybe you have an ex who treated you poorly and you find it hard to believe that a different relationship will be better. Maybe you have deep regrets from a past relationship. Maybe you lost someone or were left by someone you love.

I never knew relationships could make life so hard. I wish I had gotten a warning brochure—like you get on an airplane—before taking off into the world of dating. For me, there was the broken engagement, the friend I started to like until I realized he was secretly dating other people, the guy who was just trying to hook up with me, the guy who did not have any attention left for me after spending all his attention on himself, the guy who had his perfect future planned and thought I would drop into it without my own interests, and so many more. As I think about all those times, I realize that every single one has affected me. As much as I wish I had strong walls up to keep those situations from hurting me, I must admit they got through to my heart, my mind, my hopes, and my attitude on dating. Each experience warped and molded me to become the person I am today. A lot of character building, growth, and trust in God has happened as a result, but the good pieces have not eliminated the fear and anxiety that the bad situations have brought on.

Because of my experience with the broken engagement, it has taken years to stop assuming every person I go on a date with has some big secret that will later destroy me. Honestly, I am still working on that. The more I get to know a person, the louder the fear yells in my mind. On top of that, my past dating hurts have added up in my mind to whisper that there is something wrong with me or else I would have found my person already. They tell me everything is my fault. This fear creeps up in my mind not only in dating but it can break through to every area of my life.

When those fears come knocking at my door, I am tempted to throw out dating completely. Why open myself up to more hurt?

Why let myself continuously get rejected? Why spend copious amounts of time with someone who is not going to be in my life in a few months? It would be so easy to avoid the pain, the discomfort, and the fear that's triggered by trying to date. Life seems much easier when it is only God, my cat, and me taking on the world.

But God did not call me to live a life with the purpose of being comfortable and avoiding anything that might upset me. I do not believe that He wants me to be ruled by the fears from the past, whether it is in dating or any other area of my life. If you are struggling with your self-worth, your hopelessness in dating, or any past experience that is impeding your ability to live your best life right now, I think that you and I can both learn a lesson from our next bachelorette. She is a single woman who had incredible baggage, but God helped her through it, just like He will help you and me.

God does not want our painful past experiences to negatively define our future. He shows us a beautiful example of how He can help us unload our baggage and live a much lighter life, free from those burdens. Let's see how He does this by taking a look at our next bachelorette: Hagar.

The Bachelorette:
HAGAR

ORIGIN: Egypt
OCCUPATION: Slave
STATUS: Single mother
TALENTS: Being seen

Imagine if your life story was one people avoid telling their children because it is too difficult to explain to kids. Well, that is the reality of the life of Hagar. If you grew up in a Christian household, you were probably taught about a famous person in Hagar's life: Abraham, the father of all the generations of Israelites, the man whom God promised to send the Savior through. I bet when you learned about Abraham, you didn't hear about Hagar. I don't think it is a story that is emphasized with children, or maybe I simply had no idea what it meant as a kid.

Now that I am in my late twenties, I can appreciate Hagar's story much more than when I was five. It is incredible to think about this classic Bible tale from Hagar's perspective. We do not know much about Hagar's background besides that she was an Egyptian slave of Abraham's wife, Sarai.

While she was in service to Sarai, Abram (later called Abraham) and Sarai desperately wanted children. God directly told Abram that he would be a great nation. (I wish God would share those things with me.) But after ten years rolled by without Sarai conceiving, Abram and Sarai started to doubt God's promise and decided to take matters into their own hands. They thought they'd "help" an infinitely powerful God fulfill His promises. Never a good idea!

Sarai thought that since she was not conceiving a child, the next best thing would be for someone else to have a baby with Abram. She was extremely considerate not to bring other people into her problems—not!—and decided that her slave, Hagar, was the solution to her infertility issues.

So, what did Sarai do? She gave Hagar to Abram as a wife. Sarai's plan worked, and Hagar became pregnant with Abram's child. Now, the Bible does not provide the details of how all this transpired. Hagar was a slave so did she have a choice in this? Was she OK with it, or did she hate it? The Bible does not tell us, but it does say that when Hagar found out she was pregnant, she was not happy. "When she knew she was pregnant, she began to despise her mistress" (Gen. 16:4).

Sarai may have seen Hagar as a reflection of her own insecurity. Hagar could get pregnant from Abram, but for some reason,

Sarai could not. That may have fueled jealousy and hatred toward Hagar. Regardless of the reason, Sarai started mistreating her slave. Not only did Sarai make Hagar sleep with her husband, she now started oppressing this pregnant lady. Poor Hagar. She could not handle it, and the Bible says that Sarai mistreated her so much that it caused Hagar to flee to the desert. Imagine how bad the situation must have been that Hagar thought fleeing alone to the desert while pregnant was better than staying with Sarai. Especially when traveling alone as a woman was quite dangerous.

As pregnant Hagar was traversing the desert, what do you think was going through her mind? She was probably afraid of what would happen to her and her baby. Maybe she was somewhat relieved to be out of a toxic situation. Hagar was on the road to Shur, which was also the road to Egypt, so she was most likely attempting to return to freedom in her homeland. As she was at a spring in the desert, Hagar was visited by an angel of the Lord who asked her where she was going.

Hagar told the angel that she was fleeing from her mistress, and do you know how the angel responded?

"Go back to your mistress and submit to her" (v. 9).

What? If you were Hagar, what would you think? Words like "heck no" would be my response to that command. But in this situation, God wanted Hagar to go back to the people and place where she had been hurt. God did not want her to flee from her pain and trauma. He wanted her to address it.

Now, I wish I could say that a blanket statement of "go back to your pain and address it" just like God commanded Hagar would apply to all people in all circumstances, but I know that is untrue and inconsiderate of unique situations. There are plenty of scenarios where you should not go back, and even my counselor has told me to never meet with certain people again.

What I think we can take away from this story is that somehow Hagar was able to return to Abram and Sarai and face her pain despite all the baggage she carried from her time with them. We do not need to physically go back to our pain, but how Hagar was able to have the strength to address her pain is the piece of the story that I think can be very helpful for you and me.

LETTING GO OF THE PAST

I want you to start thinking about what baggage you might be carrying around with you. Maybe God is bringing something to your mind right now that we can work through. What things have you smushed to the back of your brain to avoid dealing with because they hurt too much to think about. For me, these are things like sins I feel I am not forgiven for, comments that made me feel unworthy, questions I am afraid to ask God, and memories that make me wake up crying in the middle of the night. There are words I have said and ways that people have treated me that I wish I could forget. It is easy to put in my headphones and try to tune out all those memories and thoughts. But the problem with avoidance is that the thoughts are a monster that we lock away. It grows stronger, and eventually it breaks out—especially when we do not want it to.

Let me give you an example. When my identity was being crushed (see chap. 1), my counselor diagnosed me with anxiety, depression, and PTSD. Counseling helped me work through so much of what was going on in my head and my heart. I reached a point where I thought I had worked past all the pain, but many years later, I realized that part of the beast was still alive, hidden in a corner of my mind.

I avoided dating for a year after breaking off my engagement. It felt wrong, and I did not enjoy the feeling of someone liking me, only for me to emotionally freak out at some trigger the poor boy had no idea about. I eventually dated a bit, had more bad experiences (we would need an entire new book for all those), stopped dating again for a few years, and eventually tried dating once again.

I honestly did not have a huge desire to try with this person, but he came very highly recommended so I caved and went on the date. There were no immediate fireworks or anything, but going on a date felt good again, which was a huge step for me. That one date turned into a couple more. This person seemed promising, and we had good times together, but in classic Hannah dating fashion, there is no such thing as "normal" dating. One weekend we met up for breakfast, and after we sat down and started talking, it felt like a bulldozer came out of nowhere and crushed me with anxiety and fear. I robotically answered some questions and then grabbed my purse and ran to the bathroom, apologizing and not knowing if I was going to have a panic attack, if my body was going to explode, or if I was going to start crying. I got to the bathroom, had a very good throw-up, did some deep breathing for a few minutes, and went "Oh no, what do I do now?" So, of course, I grabbed my purse, went back out smiling, and with the feeling of anxiety still clenching me inside, told my date, "I just threw up."

Who goes for breakfast with someone and ends up throwing up? Someone who has buried pain and misery so deep that when it attacks, it can completely take them out. At the time, I didn't understand why anxiety came on me like a tidal wave.

After some intense reflection, I realized it was one of my date's comments that triggered a deep insecurity inside of me, an insecurity I thought was gone. At breakfast, my date said that it would be emotionally draining to truly know a person and everything about them. He was not interested in that type of relationship. OK, hindsight, this was definitely not the right guy for me. That was our last date, but it helped me realize something. His comment automatically unlocked a giant piece of baggage I had been carrying around for years—the belief that no one would ever want to truly understand me and love me for who I am. The baggage was created when my engagement broke off. When we were trying to figure out what to do, I wished my fiancé and I could go back to a deeply loving and caring relationship. I craved what we used to have and the affection he used to show me, but it was all gone, plagued by the addiction. For months after we broke up, I had dreams we were together again, in perfect sync and harmony, getting ready for our wedding, only to wake up and realize that the relationship was over. I worried I would never have that deep connection with someone again—where someone saw all my flaws and thoughts and still loved me in spite of my imperfections. I feared my chance had come and gone.

Then, as I tried to date again, I had a hard time connecting with people. I wondered if I should tell them everything that had happened to me right away. How could I explain my fears and reactions? Even when I tried to explain, people struggled to connect with my life, or they started to get to know me and did not like who I truly was.

After my broken engagement, I had another very scarring dating experience that loaded more pounds into my baggage. This experience made me stop dating completely for the second time in my life. There was a guy who cared very deeply about my thoughts and emotions. He would bring me chocolate every day and ask me, "What are your concerns today and how can I help?" It doesn't sound real, right? That's way too much chocolate for one person! We grew close over a year, until we could barely put our phones down when we were apart. We had delicious dinners and talked and joked about all our thoughts and experiences. I thought he truly, deeply cared about me, right up until the point where I found out he had a wife.

That experience shook me to my core. Once again, I was incredibly deceived by a person. Once again, I felt I would never truly be known and loved by another person without them having some hidden secret.

So, years later, when I tried dating again and my date admitted to me that "completely understanding you and your emotions would be exhausting," the fears that had been festering in my mind for years were affirmed. I wondered, *Why should I keep trying? Why should I continue to waste my time dating?* All the trying, dressing up, trying to impress people by seeming like a good, interesting human being was pointless. No one would ever care for me like I longed to be cared for, and I was emotionally fragile enough in that fear that one phrase from a person I barely knew could send me to the bathroom loaded with uncontrollable anxiety.

So today I will raise my hand and admit I still have tons of baggage to work through. There are tons of mistrust, tons of insecurity, and tons of anxiety pouncing on me unexpectedly at any moment. I am giving examples related to dating, but there are plenty of other examples of triggers from past experiences that can creep into my life when I am not paying attention. Fears of losing people, fears of accidents, fears of spiders, fears of failing, and so many more that stop me from enjoying the blessing of the present moment and the present life that God has given me.

In all these situations, I have a choice. I can let my fear, anxiety, and baggage from the past run my life, or I can work to control it instead. Sure, I could try to avoid the situations that trigger the pain. I could give up dating. I could give up talking to people. I could give up leaving my house. But that is not living. If I don't address the pain, it will never go away. Maybe that is why God wanted Hagar to go back to the source of her pain. Maybe that is why God is placing something in your mind right now that He wants you to address. Hold it there as I will hold my fears, and let's take a look at how Hagar found the strength to address her pain.

After she was told to go back to Abram and Sarai, Hagar received a beautiful promise from God.

> You are now pregnant
> and you will give birth to a son.
> You shall name him Ishmael,
> for the LORD has heard of your misery.
> He will be a wild donkey of a man. (Gen. 16:11–12)

God heard Hagar in her misery, just as God hears you in your pain.

Now the last phrase—"He will be a wild donkey of a man"—is not something I would want said of a child I was pregnant with. It seems like quite a silly line, but in the historical context, it is actually quite amazing. Wild donkeys were free. They could do whatever they wanted and live however they liked. This imagery is similar to how we might picture a wild stallion running free. For God to promise Hagar—a slave who was potentially forced into motherhood—that her son would be as free as a wild stallion would have been revitalizing.

In response, Hagar said, "You are the God who sees me" (v. 13).

YOU ARE THE ONE GOD SEES

Picture Hagar taking that first step in returning to her pain. Imagine the deep breath she must have taken as she turned around and her feet started to move in the direction she came from. I am sure it would have been easy to feel like she was alone—pregnant in the desert, having to travel back to Abram and Sarai—but she knew the truth: God saw her in her pain. He was not ignoring her.

I do not know what pain and devastation haunts you, but you are not alone in fighting it. You are not alone when you are waiting for that text, throwing up during a date (or is that just me?), crying in the middle of the night, rejected by the umpteenth person, or haunted by your past tragedies. *You* are the one God sees.

God sees you in your heartache and pain. In your triggers and anxiety. You do not need to hold on to them alone. God is with you and will help you as you take those first steps to unpack the baggage you have been carrying with you. God can help you unload your baggage so you can live a free life in the beautiful present. Working through your pain will probably not be an easy process—Hagar had to literally take steps backward to get there—but I promise you, it is worth it. Let's see what happened in Hagar's story.

Knowing God saw her, Hagar was able to journey back to Abram and Sarai, whose names God then changed to Abraham and Sarah. But despite following God's command, her situation became far worse. Hagar had her baby, but then Sarah also conceived and had a baby. Since Hagar and her baby no longer served a purpose, Sarah wanted Hagar and her son out of her sight. As a result, Abraham (you know, the guy who got Hagar pregnant) sent Hagar and her son into the desert with nothing but a bit of food and a skin of water that he set on Hagar's shoulders. Ouch! Are you kidding me? He couldn't even spare a camel for the woman he got pregnant, not to mention his own son!

Hagar, once again, found herself wandering in the desert, but this time she was with her son. Once the water was gone, which probably did not take long, Hagar put Ishmael under a bush because she could not stand to see him die. Then she sat nearby and cried.

Can you imagine the pain Hagar must have felt in that moment? She did not ask for any of this. But still all these horrible things happened to her.

If I were her, I would be screaming, "Why, God? I listened to You and look how this has turned out! I faced what You told me to face and now I'm not only hurt but my son is also dying. Are You kidding me? Is this what happens when I follow You?"

The Bible says:

> God heard the boy crying, and the angel of God called to Hagar from heaven and said to her, "What is the matter, Hagar? Do not be afraid; God has heard the boy crying as he lies there. Lift the boy up and take him by the hand, for I will make him into a great nation."
> Then God opened her eyes and she saw a well of water. . . .
> God was with the boy as he grew up. (Gen. 21:17–20)

God helped Hagar face the source of her pain, and He even allowed her life to get worse after facing that pain. But look at the outcome God created for her. Hagar and her son were free. They were free from slavery, and God was with them.

So, "What is the matter, [insert your name here]?"

Can you hear God asking you this? As I was throwing up in the bathroom, God was asking, "What is the matter, Hannah?"

How do you respond to that question? What thing is God bringing up in your mind right now? For me, it was that I just wanted someone who loved me, cared about me, and understood me. Once again, I had that horrible feeling that despite my best efforts, that person was not going to care for me the way I craved. I again had to face the disappointment.

"What is the matter, Hannah?"

I'm sick of being disappointed.

"What is the matter, Hannah?"

I want to be loved.

Then came the big loving grin from God.

"I have loved you with an everlasting love. I knew you before you were created, and I will love you after the world is no more. What is the matter, Hannah?"

If God asked you that question, how would you respond? What things are preventing you from enjoying the blessings of your life? I do not want you to be pulled down by your baggage like I have let myself be pulled down so many times. Think about how you would answer the question from God. Maybe you feel OK right now, but there was something last week or last month that you wish you would have heard God asking in that moment, "What is the matter?" Maybe tomorrow, next week, or next year, something will happen where God will need to ask you, "What is the matter?"

You are unique and your past is unique, so I cannot give you some magical three-step process that will fix every single person's baggage. But what I want you to consider is this: What one thing can you do today that will help lighten your load tomorrow?

Maybe today you can work through one of your "What is the matter?" answers. You can identify one past pain or experience that haunts you in the present. Here are some steps that I like to take when I address a "What is the matter?" in my life.

1. Identify the emotion you are feeling. Identifying the emotion gives you power over it because now you know what you are facing.
2. Understand the present events that triggered the emotion. (For example, I heard a particular song on the radio and it gave me anxiety.)
3. Identify the past event that your present feelings are connected to. (For example, that song on the radio was playing when I was broken up with.) When the event happened in the past, where was Jesus in the room? What was the look on His face?
4. Remember that you are safe right now. God sees you right now and always. He is here to help you. What about your present situation gives you strength over this?
5. Talk through your "What is the matter?" with God.

You may be able to work through many of your traumas and issues alone, but it is far more wonderful to let people help. Go through the above list with a trusted friend, or, if you feel the pull, go to someone who is professionally trained to help you out. Do not dismiss counseling if it is crossing your mind. I have done it, and it was obnoxiously helpful and healing for me. My friends have done it; my family has done it. It can help change your life. I used to dismiss counseling because I thought you had to survive some apocalyptic trauma to qualify. That is simply not true. Your pain and your hurt are valid as is. You do not have to face them alone. Satan loves to isolate you so that your pain is more powerful. Do not let him win this battle.

Another thing I do when I feel my baggage overwhelming me is remind myself that I am in the present. Apparently, my brain likes to take my feelings and emotions back into the past as if I have fallen into Dumbledore's pensieve (see *Harry Potter and the Goblet of Fire*) and am experiencing the traumas and regrets again firsthand. It is a strange sensation. My friend gave me this tip to remind me that I am no longer in those situations. Use as many senses as possible to connect your brain to the present. The more senses you can use, the better. This may be lighting a candle, taking a warm bath, listening to music, or eating warm brownies and reminding yourself that you are in this moment, not the past, and you are safe here. Doing this helps me get into a mental space where it is much easier to do the five steps above.

Maybe the first step in dealing with your baggage can be the process I just described. Or maybe it is confiding your feelings in a friend. Maybe it is praying to God. Maybe it is signing up for counseling. Maybe it is digging into Bible passages specific to your pain. I pray God is giving you some idea of what that first step looks like. Set yourself up for a better life by taking it. Remember, you will not be doing this alone.

God sees you, just as He saw Hagar. God is with you. He can help you face your pain. Whatever you are dealing with—the disappointment of dating or some other extreme loss—pray that God will give you the strength to face it with Him fighting with you and for you. He can guide you to a life that is lighter. A life where you can breathe. A life where you can wake up with joy and happiness in the present. And ultimately, He is going to lead you to a life of perfect freedom from your past pain by taking you to heaven with Him for all eternity. Do not let your baggage rob today of its potential for beauty and happiness.

DIVING
DEEPER

1. What baggage are you carrying around?

2. Why is it a bad thing to carry baggage?

3. If God asked you "What is the matter?" how would you respond?

4. Which of the five steps above do you find most helpful in dealing with your baggage?

5. What does it mean to you that you are a person whom God sees?

6. How can God help you work through your baggage?

7. Why is it hard to let go of your baggage?

8. What one thing can you do today to make your baggage lighter tomorrow?

9. How does Matthew 11:28–30 help in dealing with your baggage?

5

singleness

I AM PULLED FROM MY DREAMS of flying on dragons and traveling through outer space as my alarm clock rings and my cat chimes in with his chorus of meows. The noise takes me from my cozy sleep to the harsh reality of morning. I roll over, grab my phone to turn off the alarm, and decide that I have plenty of time to get ready. I can pull up my covers and stay in my warm and comfortable bed a few minutes longer while I scroll through emails.

What is in my inbox? A flood of advertisements. There is the woman wearing the beautiful black flowing dress with the guy next to her, staring in complete admiration. There is the lady in the ridiculously uncomfortable-looking high heels who turns all the guys' heads as she walks by. There is the man who used the right shampoo and now women can't keep their hands off of his hair. There is advertisement after advertisement giving me the message that by buying the right clothes or perfect shade of lipstick, I will be happier because then I will attract someone to like me (who, of course, will be extremely good-looking).

After getting sick of these emails, I make the mistake of opening social media. As you can guess, the situation quickly spirals downward. Up pop pictures of extravagantly happy couples going for walks, getting Starbucks, kissing, buying houses, underwater basket weaving, having babies, knitting blankets, and being each other's "favorite wedding date." Everything serves as a reminder of how incredibly inadequate and unaccomplished my single life is.

I pull myself away from my phone, finally get ready for the day, then go to my car. When I turn on the radio, song after song after song after song comes on about being in love.

The emails, the social media posts, and the songs reminding me that I would be happier in a relationship all hit me before it is even 7:30 a.m. At that point, I haven't even had time to pump some caffeine into me to take on the challenges of the day.

MESSAGES FROM THE WORLD

Pay attention to your day. Is your experience similar to mine? My day is filled with subliminal messages from advertisements, movies, media, and even not-so-subliminal messages from people in my life falsely leading me to believe that happiness can be found only in a relationship. Sometimes they bog me down, but other times I am able to laugh them off.

One of the funniest examples of this happened to me a few years ago around Christmastime. When you search for something online, that information can be tracked (depending on your settings), so online advertisements are shown to you based off your previous searches. For example, if you search for party supplies, you may get advertisements for balloons and piñatas, or if you search for home decor, you may get advertisements for candles and plants.

A few years ago, I searched for Christmas toys for my cat. And do you know what advertisements I received in response? The targeted ads were not for cat food or laser toys as anticipated.

Instead, I was flooded with advertisements for dating websites. Whoever set up the advertisement thought that people who buy cat toys for Christmas are probably single and want to be in a relationship. Well played, ad companies, well played.

As funny as the examples can be, it can be pretty exhausting to constantly receive messages that our single lives are not good enough. That we would be happier if we were in a relationship. What's worse is that it is easy to believe these messages. I am guilty of buying the purse that will make men fawn over me, and I've fallen into the trap of thinking I truly will be happier if I am in a relationship.

Who decided we should view relationships as a superior status to singleness? Was it a marketing team in the eighties? While sitting at a big table late at night, chugging coffee and trying to figure out what new messaging they should pair with their product to meet sales goals, someone piped up, "What if we advertised to show that happiness is in a relationship and that relationship will happen because of our product!" Or did it come from stories told around campfires centuries ago where the tales of adventures were great, but the ultimate reward was falling in love at the end of the story? Or did these messages stem from Disney movies that promise everyone a "happily ever after" after numerous catchy songs and a picture-perfect wedding?

Regardless of where the elevated view of relationships originated, that narrative can wear us down as we try to enjoy our single lives. So what are we supposed to do with the emphasis our society puts on finding and having a significant other? Is it having the right attitude? Will that truly make us happy? Or is it simply the world trying to fill a hole in our hearts that is intended for God?

Romans 12:2 tells us, "Do not conform to the pattern of this world, but be transformed by the renewing of your mind. Then you will be able to test and approve what God's will is—his good, pleasing and perfect will."

How can we renew our minds? How should we look at our single status away from all the opinions and influences of the world: the songs, the poems, and the TV shows? Our next bachelor, Paul, can tell us the answer. He explains what our view of singleness should be when we look at it through a godly lens.

> *The Bachelor:*
> **PAUL** (formerly known as Saul)
> OCCUPATION: Former Christian persecutor, preacher of the gospel
> CITIZENSHIP: Roman
> TALENTS: Finding contentment in every situation

If you have heard a rare sermon on singleness in your church or someone talking about being single in the context of the Bible, you have probably heard of our bachelor. Paul had an incredible transformation, going from a person who was trying to capture and kill Christians to a Christian who used his entire life to proclaim God's Word. He was a great leader in the Christian church. We have many letters from him in the Bible, but one section is very important for you and me today.

In 1 Corinthians 7:7–8 Paul says, "I wish that all of you were as I am. But each of you has your own gift from God; one has this gift, another has that. Now to the unmarried and the widows I say: It is good for them to stay unmarried, as I do."

If you have heard this passage before, you may have some grief with it. I have seen this passage used many times to dismiss struggling singles because they have been blessed with "the gift of singleness" and should continue faking a smile after receiving the gift they did not want to receive. Later in this chapter, we will get into a "gift" in singleness that God has been showing me recently, but for now I want to focus on a different aspect of this passage.

This world acts like being part of a relationship or marriage is the same as getting a promotion. You have moved on to a greater and more significant life than when you were single. However, Paul tells us the exact opposite. Singleness is a good thing, and people should aspire to it! Both singleness and non-singleness are equal levels of life. Let me say that again.

Singleness and non-singleness are equal according to God! Marriage is not an achievement that makes one more qualified as a human being; it is simply a different and equally important life path.

Now you may be thinking to yourself, *Great! God views my singleness as equal to marriage, but that does not change my desire to be in a relationship and my feeling that I would be happier if I were.*

I wrestle with that same thought too. I know God views singleness and non-singleness as equal, despite how society and the people in our lives make us feel. But how do we get to a point where we truly believe singleness and marriage are equal? Especially if we want to be in a relationship?

There are many different facets to elevating marriage above singleness, and I think we owe it to ourselves to work through them. Having God's view of singleness and relationships as equal can lighten the burden we place on ourselves. It can take off the pressure of achieving the relationship "milestone." It can help us laugh at all the relationship messaging we receive instead of feeling unworthy. It can remind us that God adores our relationship status, even if our grandma does not.

So where do we begin? The first step is asking ourselves whether we have a realistic or an unrealistic view of marriage.

THE REALITY OF MARRIAGE

One of the biggest lies I have convinced myself to believe is that marriage is a perfect and magical fairy tale that will make me a better and happier person. As a kid, I had a great example of marriage in my parents. They made each other laugh, ran a family together, helped each other out, and still grossly seemed in love after raising three kids. I had their example along with all the Disney movies that showed me how amazing marriage would be—full of singing animals and dancing!

However, the reality is that marriage is a lot of hard work, and it is really hard to teach animals to sing and dance. Marriage takes two sinful people and tries to make their lives work together. I have never been married so I am only passing on information from others. If you have been married, I am sure you know this truth much better than I can possibly explain. Being married has huge blessings, but it also comes with a lot of work and requires compromise to keep the relationship healthy. My friends who are part of marriages that I greatly admire are kind enough to be honest with me and tell me, "Do not be fooled. Marriage is very difficult." Those people are committed to working every single day to make the best marriage possible. Unfortunately, that is the best side of the spectrum. The other side has couples who argue in front of me, talk about their spouse behind their back, and tell me they have massive communication problems. So many things can go wrong, and it is heartbreaking to see relationships fall apart when sin creeps in and takes over.

If you feel like you are idolizing marriage, start asking your married friends to be honest with you about their experiences. They do not need to tell you all their secrets, but hearing from couples I look up to has given me a healthy dose of reality to remind myself that marriage is not this magical thing that can fix all my problems, worries, and anxieties.

Marriage can be wonderful, but on this earth, it will never be perfect, and many times, it will probably not be easy. But the great thing about marriage—whether we are in one or not—is that it points to a true fairy tale full of happiness and fulfillment. Marriage on earth is a tiny, imperfect replica of a beautiful masterpiece showing us how much God loves us. It points to the fact that we are the bride of Christ. We have our perfect relationship with Jesus (well, perfect on Jesus's side, not ours). He gave Himself up for us, forgives us no matter what we do, always takes us back no matter how far we stray, and will take us to be with Him forever in perfect bliss. His love for us is truly infinite and greatly surpasses any human relationship.

That big picture sounds great, right? But how does it impact us on a daily basis when we are exhausted and lonely and feel like God does not care? One of my favorite reminders of my daily relationship with God is communion. I didn't know the historical context of communion until a few years ago, and it definitely makes my list of top-ten most mind-blowing things I have learned in recent years.

At the time when Jesus instituted communion, the cultural practice was for a Jewish man to propose marriage by having a dinner and gathering all his friends and family together. During the meal, he would take a cup of wine and pass it to the woman he was proposing to. If she accepted the cup and drank from it, they would be engaged. Once that happened, the man would go back to his parents' house and work on building up a home, typically one that was attached to his parents' house with rooms for his wife and him to live in.

The bride would spend this time at home with her family, not knowing the day or hour her groom would come back. She would wait in excitement for the day when her groom finished preparing a place for her so they could get married. When their home was finished, the groom would come back to take his bride—typically announced by trumpets and celebrations. Then they'd get married and go to the place that he prepared for them.[1]

Does any of that sound familiar? When Jesus offered the cup of wine to His disciples during the first communion, they may have been confused about why Jesus seemed to be proposing

---

1. Sarah Winbow, *Biblical Feasts* (Cumbria, England: New Beginnings Press, 2015), 10–11.

to them. When we take communion, it is the exact same thing. Jesus is offering us the cup, asking if He can be our "groom." He is preparing a place for us in heaven, and we can wait in anticipation until He comes back, announced by trumpets, to take us to be with Him forever. Every time I take communion, I imagine Jesus offering me the cup of wine, saying, "I choose you. Will you be mine?" And then I think how wonderful it is to be Jesus's "bride." To have a life and future with Him guaranteed for all of eternity.

That is the beautiful relationship to which earthly marriage is pointing. Being Jesus's bride means God sacrificed Himself for us, loves us infinitely, and did everything so that we could be with Him forever. And guess what? *You have God's perfect love right here and now.*

No earthly marriage can enhance that. No earthly marriage can come close to the love He has for us today.

If you tend to elevate marriage above singleness, remember that earthly marriage is not perfect, but you do have access to the relationship to which marriage points, the relationship where Jesus chooses you every single day with His infinite and endless love.

MARRIAGE LIST

Realistic view of marriage. Check. Amazing symbolism of marriage. Check. Now that we have anchored ourselves in understanding both of those aspects of marriage, we need to ask another important question. I have been working through this in order to help myself view singleness and marriage equally: "What are the specific things in marriage that I am craving and chasing after?"

My cousin once shared her list of shallow reasons for getting married. "Someone to do my taxes" and "someone to help with home repairs" were just two of the items that made the list. We laughed about this brilliant idea, and I began making my own list. The top items included:

- Someone who can kill spiders (a giant spider crawled across my legs when I was a kid and I still cannot get close to one)
- Someone to be a space heater at night
- Someone who can reach things in tall places

God truly does amazing things! I cannot say that enough. My sister had a cat who became very jealous when she got married—jealous enough to start attacking her husband. Being the good sister I am, I soon found myself with a newly adopted cat meowing around my house. And do you know what this cat can do? Not only is he a super snuggly eighteen-pound space heater that cuddles up to me at night, he also kills all the bugs in my house—including all the spiders! God provided me with a cat to take care of the first two items on my list of shallow reasons to get married. The third item can be taken care of with one of those cool arm-grabber-extender inventions or a ladder. Shallow list of reasons to get married: gone.

Realistically, though, there are plenty of nonshallow reasons why we desire marriage. Take the time right now to write down a list of the specific reasons (shallow or not) that you want to get married or be in a relationship.

1. _____

2. _____

3. _____

4. _____

5. _____

6. _____

Here is my list:

1. Love
2. Filling up the emotional bucket
3. Companionship
4. Feel important (sense of purpose)
5. Security (someone to help me if I am sick or need help)
6. Family (kiddos)

Just like I did with my list of shallow reasons for getting married, I think it is important to think through how each item on this list can be or is satisfied in my current circumstances. I will give you my examples of working through this.

Item 1: Love

One of my all-time favorite bands is Tenth Avenue North. They have a line in their song "By Your Side" that is from the perspective of God talking to us, saying, "Why are you looking for love? . . . as if I'm not enough?"[2]

Every single time I hear that line, it makes me feel like my life has gone from black and white to full color. It reminds me of the truth that I so easily forget every single day. God's love is infinite and unfathomable. Imagine you had an ocean full of water and you were sad because you wanted just one teensy tiny drop to add to that ocean. It would be incomparable. You would never know if the drop was added because what you already had was so magnificent and grand.

If you already have God, what else could you possibly need?

If you ever struggle with feeling unloved like I do, spend some time in awe of God's love for you. Read Psalm 36:5–7, John 3:16, Romans 8:35–39, and Ephesians 3:18–19—but honestly, you

---

2. Tenth Avenue North, "By Your Side," *Over and Underneath*, Provident Label Group LLC, 2007 compact disc.

might as well just read the entire Bible. Another thing you can do is think of how many people God has given you in your life that love you. Make a list of every person you can think of, and be overwhelmed by just one example of how God shows His love for you.

Item 2: Filling Up the Emotional Bucket

It is easy for me to ignore my emotional bucket until it is completely empty. I often sit on the couch staring off into space, too afraid to move because then I will need to confront the mountain of things I need to get done. I feel too emotionally exhausted and drained to do even tiny tasks, like texting someone back or putting dishes in the dishwasher.

I like to believe that having a significant other would help me avoid reaching this zombie state. I would have someone to laugh and cry with. I would have someone with whom I can do things that fill me up, like hiking, eating amazing food at restaurants, seeing Broadway musicals, going quiet clubbing at the art museum, having deep conversations, building forts, and dreaming about the future. Without that significant other, I am bad at stopping to take time to relax and enjoy life.

But I do not need a significant other to pay attention to filling up my emotional bucket, and you do not need one either. I have started to pay attention to the things that replenish me. They may seem small, but when I stop doing them, I find myself drifting into emotional comatose. When I make time to replenish myself, it is much easier to take on the challenges of the day. Here are the items that have helped to fill me up:

1. Morning Routine

Do something before you start work or school that makes you excited to wake up in the morning. It might be taking twenty minutes to slowly drink your coffee in the quiet of the day as the sun rises. It might be going for a walk in the fresh air with no one around. It might be doing a devotion, journaling, or working out. Instead of immediately diving into the chaos of the day, find something that gives you your own time to think and wake up in the morning.

2. Nighttime Wind-Down

Just like the morning, give yourself time to enjoy being you before you go to bed. You repeat similar activities from the morning routine: drink a warm cup of chamomile tea, grab a good book, journal about your day, write stories, knit, read the Bible, or anything else that will help you unwind and relax before bed.

If you feel like you do not have time in the morning or at night, start off small. Try taking just five or ten minutes to have some time to yourself to decompress. You can always add more later.

3. Single Dates

Just because we are single does not mean we cannot go on dates. We can go on single dates! For so long I did not want to go places by myself. I thought people would judge me for being alone and give me strange looks. But then one day a movie was playing at the local film festival that I wanted to see, and none of my friends could go. I was faced with the dilemma: should I go by myself and potentially feel awkward or stay home and miss it?

I decided to go but was nervous and felt so awkward about it that I'm surprised I made it to the theater. As I waited in line for a ticket, there was an older woman next to me who was also alone. Somehow we started up a conversation. As we waited, we talked about our careers and lives. I was insanely impressed with this woman. She was a breast surgeon and told me about her school, her family, her role in fighting breast cancer, and so many interesting things! When we got to the counter, she paid for my ticket, asked me to sit by her, and then also paid for my dinner after the show. It was a phenomenal night!

That experience filled up my emotional bucket. As singles we are often pulled into what groups or couples want to do, so it is extremely important to take the time to do the things we enjoy. You can do this by planning single dates for yourself. Plan a date to the movies, the museum, the park, the fancy restaurant, or the concert. It might be going dancing, going to a painting class, or going hiking. Get regular massages to raise the oxytocin in your brain. Give yourself something to look forward to that is going to give you time to explore your interests and enjoy being the person God created you to be. Start by planning a single date once a month, and then increase it from there as you get used to it.

Item 3: Companionship

I can talk to God twenty-four hours a day, seven days a week. I have yet to meet a human who does not need sleep and can be available always like God is available to me. But God does not stop there. He has blessed me with family, friends, coworkers, the checkout lady at the grocery store, the neighbor who walks his dog past my house every day, the receptionist who schedules my vet appointments, the person who emails me because they are my distant relative and are trapped in another country and need my credit card number to get out, and so many more people to experience life with. I'm an introvert, so when I think about just how many companions God has given me, it becomes quite overwhelming, and I want to stay at home because that is way too many people.

God has provided people in our lives so that we don't have to do everything alone. If you have a serious medical appointment, bring a friend or family member to support you. If you have a house project, invite someone over to help. Schedule regular dinners with people, and fill up your companionship cup with the people God has blessed you with.

If you are longing for more companionship right now, I would encourage you to push yourself just a little outside of your comfort zone. You can start with small steps: have a conversation with the person in the checkout line next to you. Or you can push yourself further by joining a group that enjoys one of your hobbies (indoor soccer, beach volleyball, band, knitting class, etc.). Ask people at work or school to do something fun. Join a small group at church. Seek out mentors, and mentor people in turn. Join a professional organization associated with your career or professional interests. I belong to the Society of Women Engineers, for example. No one needs to be an island. Pray to God to provide the right people in your life to get that feeling of companionship filled, and go out there and start meeting people.

Item 4: Feel Important (Sense of Purpose)

This has been a hard lesson for me to learn, but no significant other can give me a true and lasting sense of importance or purpose. Another person may be able to build me up, but they will have bad days too, and if I rest my entire importance on them, I will fall down with them. The only way for me to understand my real importance and purpose is by building the right foundation in my heart. That comes from the fact that God loves me so much that out of the billions of people in the world, He still knows me by name. He has given me a purpose to spread His Word and be a light reflecting His love.

What's even cooler is that He has uniquely wired each of us to do that in a different way. We will dive into this concept in later chapters, but only God can satisfy our need to be important and have a purpose.

Item 5: Security (Someone to Help Me if I Am Sick or Need Help)

Recently, I had car issues. That phrase alone makes me cringe. It crossed my mind that a boyfriend would be very helpful in the situation where I could not get my car to even start by myself. With no helpful boyfriend riding in on a horse, I had to turn to others. In the course of three days, I had the help of numerous coworkers, complete strangers, neighbors, family members, and people from my church group helping me with my car.

I am very guilty of isolating myself and throwing a pity party about how I have to do everything alone. But then, when I am forced into a situation, like dealing with a broken car, I am obliged to realize how many people God has placed in my life to help me. Maybe you do not live in the Midwest, where if your car spins into a ditch on a snowy day, twenty strangers will stop to make sure you are OK while giving you a blanket, hot chocolate, and snacks, but I am sure that God has placed people in your life to help you when trials come your way. If you are like me, you probably have far more people than you realize.

Item 6: Family (Kiddos)

I always imagined I would have kids by now, but I am not even remotely close to being able to get pregnant. Even though I do not have my own children, God has provided me with plenty of kids to fill that void. Right now, I have four adorable nieces and nephews who warm my heart with giant smiles and run over for a hug whenever they see me. I also volunteer at my church's youth group. There are many kids in my life, and after a lot of time with them, I feel blessed that I can leave them with their parents and get a good night's sleep, trusting God will give me my own kids if and when the time is right.

That is my list of reasons to get married. When I work through my list and see what God has provided, or what steps I can take to feel satisfied in each area, my desire for marriage seems far less overwhelming. God truly has given me what I need and has even filled the gaps of what I want.

What does working through your list look like? Maybe your list is similar to mine, or maybe you had completely different items to work through. Go through your list and see what God has already done for you and what areas you may be able to do something about so the sting of singleness is taken away. I pray that by going through your list, you will see that God has provided what you need—and in fact, I bet He has provided so much more beyond that.

I believe that almost every single item on your list can be satisfied by doing this exercise. However, I am aware there are a few exceptions you will need to dive deeper on. One of the big ones is physical intimacy. I will have a lot of questions for God on this one when I get to heaven. It is quite tricky to understand what to do with the sex drive wired in us when we are single. For some people, it is only annoying thoughts that creep into their minds on occasion, but for other people, the thoughts never really seem to go away. Even with this list item, though it seems more difficult to satisfy, I think God has given us the means to address our desire for physical intimacy while we are single. It just takes hard work. If this is a big struggle for you, please look into the many books, podcasts, counselors, and people who can help you in this area. There is a plethora of information out there, but I am going to give you two tips that I believe can help you get started.

The first thing I recommend is that you figure out when sexual thoughts come into your mind. If you start to analyze when you desire physical intimacy, you may notice a pattern, such as times you are stressed out and want an escape, times you are bored, times you are lonely, times you want someone to care about you, times you want to feel something, or times you are angry. Yes, it seems that physical intimacy could easily and very temporarily help those situations, but that would only be putting a Band-Aid on a critical wound and would not fix those feelings. You need to get at the root of what is really causing the feelings. Then, instead of turning to a behavior you might regret to numb your feelings (like pornography), you can figure out how to address the issue. If you use sex to numb yourself when you are single, you will never work through the problems in your mind. If God does have marriage in your future, your brain will be wired to use that other person you love as a drug for your relief from the issues you have not worked through. You owe it to yourself not to make either of those situations the reality of your life. You are the one who God chooses every day. If you struggle with this area, start taking steps to make a change.

The other piece of advice I have is to talk to someone you trust. A common pattern I have seen when it comes to sexual sins is that someone struggles, sins, feels terrible about themself, which causes them to struggle more, then fall into the sin more. This cycle continues as they think they are a terrible person and are in the fight alone. They cannot imagine sharing their struggle because they are so ashamed of it. But guess what? That is the exact way Satan wants you to feel: horrible about yourself and completely alone.

Do not give in. I have been honored when friends have trusted me enough to share the struggles of their sexual sins with me. Let me tell you what that looks like. A friend will be brave enough to share with me what they are going through, and it does not make me view them as a worse person. I love them even more because they were able to open up about their struggle. Then God gives me the awesome opportunity to assure them that they are forgiven and that I am there to help them and pray with them as they work through their struggle. It is amazing to see how much the relief of stress lightens someone's face after having those conversations. Please, confide in someone. Do not struggle alone. So many people are going through what you are, and you will feel so much relief when you share your burden.

THE BIG PICTURE

Now that we have taken a realistic look at marriage and examined our own reasons for wanting to get married, let's look at one more important piece of information that will help us stop being squeamish when we read Paul's words about having the "gift" of singleness.

There are some days when I slave away at work for hours and hours, staring at the computer screen in front of me. I am so consumed in doing work that I barely let my eyes leave the screen—even to look at the food I'm eating for lunch.

Then, at the end of the day, I get up to leave, and as I walk to my car, I notice an interesting thing happening. I have a very hard time focusing on anything that is not the same distance from me as my computer screen was. I try to read signs that are far away, but they are all a blur. My eyes were so focused on what was immediately in front of me that I can barely understand what is far away, no matter how hard I squint.

I do this at work, but it is so similar to what I do in my life as well. I get so focused on my worries, my fears, the things right in front of me, that I forget my life is part of a much bigger picture.

I am especially guilty of doing this when it comes to singleness. It haunts my thoughts of the present, it haunts my thoughts of the future, and it feels like there is no way to see life besides through the single lens. If you do this, too, let me show you the big picture. Here is a depiction of what our single lives look like in the scheme of eternity:

$$\longrightarrow$$

See that really small dot at the beginning of the line? No? That is because that is how small the amount of time you spend in your season of singleness will look compared with the rest of your existence.

We spend a very small fraction of time here on earth that is going to grow more and more microscopic as we spend our eternity in heaven. When you are in heaven—feasting in glorious bliss and Jesus hugs, feeling completely whole and completely loved every single moment—how do you think you will feel about the season of singleness you are going through right now? What is your short season of singleness compared with an eternity of perfect happiness?

Since singleness is just a teensy tiny fraction of our lives, when you go to heaven, do you want to admit to Jesus that you spent the majority of your days stressing out and pursuing a relationship that would last for—what?—sixty to eighty years at most. Or instead, do you want to trust that God knows what is best for your life and live fully to His calling for your years on earth? The choice of how you want to live today is yours. You have an eternity of happiness before you. Are you willing to make the most of right now by serving and trusting God, no matter what your relationship status?

If so, God has been showing me a really extraordinary facet of singleness that I never realized until recently: *Singleness gives us a unique opportunity to be a reflection of God's love.*

People in the world think that you need to be in a relationship to be happy. Since we are not supposed to be like the world, we have a great opportunity to flip that idea on its head and let our lights shine.

When people used to ask me if I was dating anyone, I would feel this huge pang of embarrassment as I awkwardly answered no and tried to explain that I was normal even though I was single. But as my view on singleness has been changing—as I am beginning to see how wonderful it truly is—I now can answer, "Yes, I am single!" with confidence, happiness, and a big smile.

Being excited about singleness is not something the world is used to. As people see you live a life full of joy, they will start to wonder how you can be so happy in a situation that to them may not be a positive one. Sometimes they may even ask you how you can be so excited about singleness. Then you can have a conversation with them about how you have God and you need nothing else to be happy. You can show them that with your life. Singleness is truly a great gift God has given us to let our lights shine into the world. For me, this has been a massive opportunity to spread some Jesus love, and I hope it can be for you as well.

DIVING
DEEPER

1. Who or what puts external pressure on you to believe that marriage is better than singleness?
2. What can you do to eliminate some of those pressures?
3. What are some pros and what are some cons of marriage?
4. What are the top reasons you want to get married? How has God provided for you in those areas? What can you do to fulfill them while you are single?
5. How do you think you will feel about your season of singleness when you are in heaven?
6. How can you use your singleness to better grow your relationship with God?
7. What are some ways you can use your singleness to let your light shine?

6

choice

AFTER I GRADUATED FROM COLLEGE, my childhood best friend and I spent a month and a half backpacking through six different countries in Europe. We visited Platform 9¾ in London, saw the church where my friend's grandpa was baptized in Leipzig, drank Guinness at a brewery in Dublin, ate one-euro-a-scoop ice cream and chocolate croissants constantly, and experienced the beautiful culture and towns of our European friends. All those days are such treasured memories to me, but as with all travels, we also ran into the occasional snafu.

One day, after we'd had our fill of schnitzel and spaetzle, we were riding on a train through Munich, Germany. I was gazing out the window, enjoying the sights of the city, when I looked around the train car and became nervous. I nudged my friend as I tried to hold in my panic. "Why are we the only ones on this train?"

We looked up and down through the windows to the other cars and realized we were completely alone. When did everyone get off the train? How did we not notice that everyone else got off? Was this going to be similar to a movie where we got drugged and were taken to some villainous place?

As the questions raced through my mind, the train slowly began to stop as it went into a dark underground tunnel. It spookily reached a full halt in a dim passageway. The doors on the train compartment remained closed. I went up to one and tried to open it, but to my distress, it was locked shut. My friend was calm and figured the train was switching directions, but as the minutes ticked by, I feared that the German announcement I did not understand may have been saying that the train cars were being taken out of commission. We would be trapped in this tunnel underground with no food, no water, and worse, no bathroom.

I looked at the red emergency button by the door. My friend and I had been backpacking through Europe for a few weeks at this point, and I had already had some grief with those buttons. I accidently hit one in the bathroom of a different train, thinking it was the "flush" button. (Apologies to all my European friends for being a very stereotypical American tourist.)

This time, I was much more cautious about hitting the red button. When I felt like enough time had passed with no one coming to our rescue, I hit it. Nothing happened. As we waited and waited, we hit the button a couple more times. No response. We were stuck, and I was panicking.

I went through every spy movie I could think of that had guidance on how to get out of these kinds of situations. *Do I break a window and try to get out? Do I find an electrical panel and force the doors open? Do I stick a watch with a bomb in it to the doors to blast them open?* As the solutions pulsed through my mind, a glorious sight appeared outside our train car. The conductor was walking outside. We pounded on the window, and she came up to our car and asked, "Didn't you hear? I said last stop. I'm turning the train around now."

Relief. We would not be trapped on a train in a dark German tunnel forever. The train began to move backward, we realized we missed our stop previously, and we got off on the correct stop to tour the FC Bayern soccer stadium on a lovely day where we met fellow Packer fans.

RELAX, IT WILL ALL WORK OUT

It is funny to think about that story now, but when I was experiencing it, I had no idea how it would end. If I had taken a breath, I could have calmly realized that trains *do* need to turn around at some point, but I let my panic and fear overtake me. This is especially humiliating because just a week before this incident, my friend and I found ourselves trapped on a different train. (Do not travel with us if you want to avoid train entrapment!) We were traveling to Salzburg, Austria, where *The Sound of Music* was filmed. Picture beautiful mountains, an old castle, extremely kind Austrians, and a hostel that played *The Sound of Music* every single night. As we journeyed to Austria, this train also came to a halt much earlier than anticipated. After listening to some announcements, we learned that a burning bush was blocking our path. Since God was apparently talking to Moses on the train tracks, we could not pass. We were stuck with no idea when we would be able to keep moving.

In this situation, I did not panic. My friend got us drinks and snacks, and we spent the passing hours doing everything from pretending we were on the Hogwarts Express to dreaming about our future travels and laughing about the pet-sitting company called PetLovers we had created as kids. I have no idea how many hours actually passed, but we were happy and content despite being stuck on a train.

To be honest, comparing these two experiences is quite embarrassing for me. On one train, I was stuck but was able to make the most of it. On the other train, I was also stuck, but I panicked and that clouded me from enjoying the time and the place I was in. Even if it was a tunnel in Germany, it was still Germany with my childhood best friend.

Being trapped on a train in Europe is one situation I have found myself in far too many times, but that is not the only experience that left me feeling stuck. I have felt trapped in pain when my body would not let me have relief from some unknown cause. I have felt trapped in sorrow when I have lost someone. I have felt trapped in singleness and pounded on the doors for God to let me out or give me an explanation.

In chapter 3, we talked about being confined in a waiting room and knowing God is working for our good in that place. Right now, I want to dive in to one more aspect of being in that waiting room, and that is our attitudes when we feel stuck in a situation in life that we do not want to be in.

The Bible offers many examples of people being trapped physically, emotionally, and even in certain life situations. One of my personal heroes in this category is Joseph. Joseph was trapped in situation after situation, but the way he was able to live his life while "trapped" has been a great inspiration for me—especially when I feel stuck in my single relationship status. Let's take a look at our next bachelor.

The Bachelor:
JOSEPH

TALENTS: Favorite son, interpreting dreams
FAMILY: Eleven angry men
LOOKS: Fashionable, especially coats

Joseph's life story was so incredible that there are numerous movies, a cartoon, and even a musical about it. He has a true underdog story. He was sold into slavery and then he eventually rose to become second-in-command in Egypt, saving his family and a multitude of other people from famine.

I can't remember the first time I learned about Joseph, but I have to imagine that little me was sitting in suspense as terrible thing after terrible thing happened to him before things took a positive turn. But when I hear his story now, it is easy to skim past all the excruciating and terrible details. But lately, I have been realizing something. Joseph lived through every hard experience with no idea where it would lead him. Really trying to put myself in Joseph's shoes (or sandals) gives me a profound respect for his response to hardship, especially because he had no idea that his pain would ever end. So, let's take a look at Joseph's story and imagine what it must have felt like to be him.

Joseph started off life in a pretty great situation: He was the favorite child of a father who loved him so much that he went to the local mall and did not buy him the denim jacket nor the leather jacket nor the fur coat nor the track jacket. No, his father got him the majestic coat of many colors. Can you picture it up on a display mannequin with lights on it and security guards surrounding this premium, luxury, designer-brand coat? And what's even more significant is that Joseph had eleven brothers, but his father got only one coat, and it was for Joseph.

Now if you were Joseph's brother, how would that make you feel? You are going around in a poncho and your brother gets the mother of all coats from your father. As I am sure you can imagine, his brothers were filled with jealousy. And to make matters worse, Joseph was sharing his dreams that these brothers would eventually all bow down to him. Joseph was better dressed, *and* he was dreaming he was going to rule over his brothers. They were not happy.

One day, all the brothers were out in the fields, tending a flock of sheep, when Joseph came strolling along. That jealousy and hatred they had been harboring sparked when they saw Joseph, and they said, "Come now, let's kill him and throw him into one of these cisterns and say that a ferocious animal devoured him" (Gen. 37:20).

Reuben was the only one who would not stand for hurting Joseph, and he told his brothers not to carry out their murderous plan. Perhaps that is why a delicious sandwich is named after him. So when Joseph came, instead of killing him, the brothers took off his designer coat and threw him into an empty cistern (see vv. 23–24). Then they saw a caravan of Ishmaelites traveling to Egypt and decided to sell Joseph as a slave (vv. 25–28).

Time to step into the mind of Joseph. What do you think was going on in his noggin at this point? Joseph was seventeen when all this happened. He probably had dreams of how his life would turn out: getting married, having little Josephs and Josephinas, and being blessed by his father at every step. But in the course of a single day, he went from a position of honor to being sold into slavery. He was forced to go away from the favor of his father, away from his home, and into an unknown and seemingly dismal future.

Maybe Joseph stayed strong during this time or maybe he hit a breaking point. Maybe he waited hopefully for his father to rescue him in those first few days but he grew more and more hopeless as time passed. We can ask him in heaven. But for now, we have only what the Bible says, and what it tells us is the opposite of what I would expect. If this were my story, the next scene would pan to me crying on the floor, upset about how my life turned out or trying to run away from captivity.

But that is not the case. The next time we see Joseph, he is in Egypt, serving Pharaoh's captain of the guard, Potiphar. Despite still being a slave, Joseph was thriving:

> The Lord was with Joseph so that he prospered, and he lived in the house of his Egyptian master. When his master saw that the Lord was with him and that the Lord gave him success in everything he did, Joseph found favor in his eyes and became his attendant. Potiphar put him in charge of his household, and he entrusted to his care everything he owned. From the time he put him in charge

of his household and of all that he owned, the LORD blessed the household of the Egyptian because of Joseph. The blessing of the LORD was on everything Potiphar had, both in the house and in the field. So Potiphar left everything he had in Joseph's care; with Joseph in charge, he did not concern himself with anything except the food he ate. (39:2-6)

Joseph was not crying, "It's so unfair that my life turned out this way!" He was persevering, and he was letting his light shine to the people around him. God blessed him—maybe not in the way Joseph would have wanted (by giving him freedom). But God blessed him in what he was doing, and God had blessings in store for his future as well.

Joseph was rocking his slave life when his story took another turn for the worse. He was single, and I have to guess he experienced a little bit of loneliness and trauma after he was ripped away from the loving part of his family by the hating part of his family. Combine Joseph's potential loneliness with the fact that Potiphar's wife had her eyes on him, and what do you get? Nothing. Joseph resisted temptation when Potiphar's wife tried to sleep with him. Even if he was lonely, he still decided to follow God instead of giving in to self-pity or desire.

Good job, Joseph. But Potiphar's wife was not happy at being rejected and had watched enough crime shows to know how to frame Joseph. She claimed he had tried to sleep with her but that she had gotten away.

As a result of Potiphar's wife's false claims, Joseph was thrown into prison. And this was not just any prison. This was where Pharaoh's prisoners were confined (insert agonizing yells).

Sold into slavery by family. Check. Thrown into prison due to false accusations. Check. Despairing situation. No check. Despite going from a slave to a prisoner, Joseph once again trusted God and worked hard in prison. God blessed Joseph so that he was put in charge of everyone and everything that was done in the prison.

One day, he noticed two of the inmates were in despair so he talked to them and interpreted their dreams. He told one of the men, Pharaoh's former cupbearer, that he would be restored to his old position. He told the other man, Pharaoh's former baker, that he was going to be killed. (I guess he must have made a pretty terrible pastry!) Both of Joseph's interpretations came true, but when the cupbearer went back to Pharaoh, he forgot about Joseph.

Two years later, with Joseph still in prison, Pharaoh had a few dreams about some cannibalistic cows and grain that no one could explain. The cupbearer finally remembered that a guy in prison had interpreted a dream for him, so he told Pharaoh and Pharaoh brought Joseph before him.

Joseph interpreted Pharaoh's dreams, making sure to give credit to God (41:25). He told Pharaoh there would be seven years of abundance in Egypt followed by seven years of famine. Joseph even went as far as to tell Pharaoh how to save his people from the coming famine. Now how did Joseph know how to help Pharaoh in this situation? How did he have this insight and expertise? (1) God was with him; (2) God was helping him; (3) God allowed Joseph to go through circumstances to prepare him for this future. I have to imagine that all the time that Joseph spent as a slave, learning how to take care of a household and run it, followed by all the time Joseph ran the prison, was God's way of teaching and preparing him for what would come next—taking care of a country. Even in the hardship, God was working everything for the good of Joseph.

The rest of Joseph's happily ever after came when Pharaoh made Joseph his second-in-command and Joseph successfully led Egypt through the famine. That food even fed Joseph's own family. Joseph not only reunited with his family in forgiveness but he also became the means to keep them alive. And most importantly, he kept the line of Judah alive, from which the Savior would come.

All these blessings were born from an insanely hard life. Joseph became second-in-command of Egypt when he was thirty years old (wow, do I feel underaccomplished!). God allowed him to go through terrible circumstances for thirteen years, but Joseph did not allow misery to rule his life, even though, I would argue, he had a very good reason to do so. Instead of succumbing to disappointment, Joseph chose to make the most out of the difficult scenarios. God was right there with him, helping him and blessing him. After he left his season of singleness, Joseph even named his second son Ephraim, which means, "It is because God has made me fruitful in the land of my suffering" (v. 52).

CHOICES, CHOICES, CHOICES

What an inspiring life! Now, let's take a look at our own stories. Every single day, just like Joseph, we have a choice to make. Here are our two options.

Option 1: We can be disappointed that things have not turned out the way we hoped and allow that misery to rule our lives. We can live like there is always a shadow over us, telling us that we would be happier if God would give us the life we wanted, a life where we fall in love and marry our dream person. With a hole in our heart, no achievement, no milestone, and no friend can make us happy because those are not the things we long for. We tell ourselves, *I have the right to be upset every single day, because I am stuck being single.* We can let that disappointment plague our thoughts and actions so that we become completely idle in our season of singleness, making excuses like, "My life is harder because I do not have a significant other to help me." With that attitude, our focus solely becomes changing our situation— spending all our time obsessing over how to leave our season of singleness. We ignore the happiness of a wedding because we are looking for someone to date, we feel sad on Christmas because we are alone, and we are upset with our friends for choosing their spouse over us. We can ignore God's calling to us here on earth and focus on trying to get the life we think we are entitled to. The life we *think* will make us happy. Maybe someday we will get married, or maybe we never will. Either way, all the years of singleness will be years where we never allowed ourselves to be truly happy and prosper in the life we have.

Option 2: We can be disappointed that our lives have not turned out the way we hoped, but we can be like Joseph and decide to persevere in our season of singleness. We know God is with us. We know God is allowing us to be stuck in this situation, so we are going to work through our negative thoughts and feelings with God, and then prosper in the season He has put us in—using our talents and our time to bring God glory and trusting in His timing and His plan. It may take some time, but we will be happy, knowing God is working in us and through us in the special place that He has put us, and knowing God has placed us here for His special purpose.

So, which option do you choose?

Option 2 is clearly the better choice, but I am guessing you agree with me that it is hard to live out. Maybe you have moments when you are content being single. You wake up in the morning with a theme song in your head, feeling pumped for the day and your life. But then a social media notification comes in, showing you that your ex is happily in a relationship, or you get a package in the mail that needs two people to lift, or a coworker asks if you are dating anyone and they react like you just told them you had cancer when you say you are single. Then they mumble something like, "Oh, I'm sorry. I shouldn't have asked," and quickly get out of the conversation. The pity-party music comes into your head as you slide back to Option 1, feeling sorry for yourself and wanting your relationship status to change. Then the sad thoughts start to overwhelm: *Everyone else has a significant other, so their life is easier. Other people don't have to do everything on their own. It's not fair that I am single.*

But every single day, you and I have the choice to either live in the sorrow of Option 1 or the joy of Option 2. It all comes down to our attitude and our willingness to take the steps to stay in the latter. Otherwise life could pass by in the sadness of Option 1, and no one deserves that.

A few years ago, I was drowning in stress at my job. I had taken a position out of college that I thought was going to be the start of my career path, but I quickly realized it was not the right fit for me. I did not enjoy the work and had to shut my office door far too frequently so no one would hear me cry from the politics of work. One Monday evening, as I was riding the elevator down to my car, I was debating if I should quit my job or not. The elevator stopped and an older woman got in, looking frustrated. I smiled and said hello.

She half smiled back and grumbled, "Another Monday over."

"Bad day?" I asked.

"I hate my job," she replied.

"How long have you been doing it?"

"Thirty years."

"And has it always been this way?" I asked.

"Yes."

I was in shock. "So why don't you change jobs?"

"At this point, what difference does it make?"

That conversation was perfect validation for me that quitting and changing something in my life was the right step. I could have stayed in my job and been like that lady, never making a change and continuing to live in misery, but I chose to do the hard thing. I put in the effort and let myself step into the unknown to make my life better, and I am so glad I did.

It's your choice to either let the weight of your circumstances crush you every day or to use that weight to get stronger so that over time, the weight is no longer heavy for you. You can now use it for God's glory.

God used difficult circumstances to prepare Joseph for a bright, meaningful, and impactful future. But Joseph, with the help of God, still strove, worked hard, and shined for God, leading to the happy ending.

I pray that you wake up every day and choose Option 2. I pray that you strive to make Option 2 your normal way of life. If your choice is to step outside your known comfort zone, leave your misery behind, and take the leap to embrace this life that God has given you, here are the first few steps you can take:

1. **Know** that God is with you just like He was with Joseph in every situation he faced.
2. **Accept** that God is letting you dwell in these life circumstances even if you do not want to be in them.
3. Since God has allowed you to come to this circumstance and He is with you, what are you capable of? **Take the leap and see.**

The next chapters will explore what that leap looks like in finding and living out your potential in your season of singleness. It is a truly beautiful place to live.

DIVING DEEPER

1. Do you fall into periods of feeling sorry for yourself? Why does that happen, and how do you think God feels about your pity party?
2. What was the most difficult part of Joseph's life?
3. Have you ever looked back at hard times, after you got through them, and realized something greater came out of them than if you hadn't gone through them?
4. Do you fall into Option 1 or Option 2 more? Why?
5. Why is it difficult to have a positive attitude about singleness?

6. What comfort does God give you in singleness?

7. How do Jeremiah 1:5, Jeremiah 29:11, John 17:15–18, and 1 Peter 2:9 give you comfort for the place you are in life right now?

8. How can you make the most of your present circumstances from the time you wake up to the time you go to bed? Look at your schedule and see how you can fully live for God.

7

time

You DEFINITELY should not read the Bible.

You have so many important things to do in your life. Why waste even ten minutes of your precious 1,440 minutes each day to dive into Scripture? You have better ways to spend your time, like watching cat videos, or cleaning your whole house, and what better time than now to organize that closet you haven't touched in two years?

The Bible is just an old book as intimidating as a classic Russian novel—full of long names of people and places that are hard to keep track of. It is far too complicated for you to understand, and if you did read the Bible, you could interpret it wrong! Why risk that danger? Sure, there are plenty of resources available—YouTube videos, websites, and commentaries—but those could have false doctrine, and that is even more dangerous than not reading the Bible. It is best to leave God's Word to the experts like pastors, small group leaders, and that angry guy posting on social media.

Plus, the Bible is so old, how could it possibly be relevant to you in your unique life? Sure, God is a genius so His Word applies to anyone born in any year and any circumstance, but that can't possibly apply to *you*.

And prayer? With all the distractions in the world, how is that even possible? There is no better expert than you to get through the pain and struggles you face each day. Why consult the God who knows your whole mind, created you, and wants what is best for you? You are obviously going to make a better choice without His guidance. Just because God is lovingly and kindly listening to your every word does not mean you need to talk to Him.

So obviously spending time with God is just about the biggest waste of time ever. You should continue prioritizing your workouts, your knitting, your baking, your memes, your sleeping in, your TV show binge-watching, your mimosas, and your comfort over any quality time with God.

Those thoughts may be a little too ridiculous and sarcastic compared with what may go through your mind, but do you find yourself struggling to make time for God? It is so easy for me to formulate excuse after excuse of why I should not spend quality time with God. I get so consumed in my day and in my life that weeks and months can pass before I realize how much dust has collected on the Bible study book I was going to read. It is easy to spend hours watching my favorite TV show, but then when I try to read the Bible at night, I can get through only a few sentences before falling asleep. I might make a New Year's resolution to read the Bible in a year, but when my social life and work become busy, that plan is the first thing to go.

It is very frustrating to think over how many times I have failed in this area of my life. So much so that when I hear the story of our next bachelorette, it is easy to roll my eyes at myself and cringe like a naughty child caught doing the wrong thing. Our next bachelorette was an expert at quality time with God, so let's take a look at how this fellow human was able to overcome the distractions and pulls of daily living in order to make time with God an important part of her life. This is not only a practice God loves but as this bachelorette will show us, committing to this can make our lives significantly lighter and freer.

The Bachelorette:
MARY

HOMETOWN: Bethany
FAMILY: Martha and Lazarus
TALENTS: Choosing what is best

Mary was the sister of Martha who opened up her home to Jesus and His disciples as they were traveling. When their guests arrived, the two sisters took the exact opposite approaches with their company: Mary planted herself at Jesus's feet so that she could listen to everything He had to say. Martha became immersed in preparations for her guests. She was cleaning, creating the charcuterie board, putting the icing on the cake, creating a Pinterest-worthy centerpiece, and making sure that every detail was perfect. Martha became consumed with these preparations, and I can picture her casting a glare at her sister who was sitting around doing nothing to help. Martha took a pause from her hosting activities to complain to Jesus.

> "Lord, don't you care that my sister has left me to do the work by myself? Tell her to help me!"
> "Martha, Martha," the Lord answered, "you are worried and upset about many things, but few things are needed—or indeed only one. Mary has chosen what is better, and it will not be taken away from her." (Luke 10:40–42)

I feel intense sympathy for Martha in this scenario. When I have hosted parties at my home, I have realized that it is a true art form to prepare a hot meal, while still talking to guests and not completely ignoring them in order to be hospitable. If Jesus was my guest, I would feel even more pressure to make the perfect meal (unless He told me He was going to provide some fish and loaves or make my water into wine). But what did Jesus care about? He did not care about all the perfect and meticulous preparations. He just wanted Mary and Martha to sit at His feet and listen to Him. It seems so simple. It seems so easy.

I don't know about you, but this section of Scripture is pure conviction for me. Even right now as I am studying it, I feel the pressure to do laundry, pay my bills, finally figure out my retirement accounts, write thank-yous, clean my messy kitchen, and tidy up my other rooms. It is so hard to get away from the endless list of tasks that only seems to multiply every time I cross something off. Taking care of my home is not the only thing on the list. It also includes plenty of tasks that make me feel like I am serving Jesus: organizing volunteers, preparing a Bible study, teaching youth group, and so many more things. My list is endless. It seems that even what I think is "serving Jesus" can get in the way of me actually sitting at His feet and listening to Him.

If you are a Mary in this story, feel free to skip the rest of this chapter. But if you are a Martha like me, we definitely have some things we can improve on together. How can we be more like Mary and put aside our busy lives and calendars to make time to sit with Jesus? Mary definitely had plenty to do, and people—like her sister, Martha—expected things from her, but she was still able to prioritize her time with God instead of giving in to the demands of the world.

So, what was Mary's secret? Was she actually just lazy and did not want to help her sister, or was there something much deeper going on in her heart? We can get a glimpse of it by revisiting the story of her brother, Lazarus. Let's look at one other small snippet in time that shows Jesus's and Mary's relationship.

In chapter 3, we dug into the story of Mary and Martha's brother, Lazarus. Today I want to reemphasize one part of that story. As I am sure you can imagine, Mary was overcome with grief when her brother died. She was mourning for Lazarus, but when Jesus showed up, she instantly went to Him and fell at His feet (must be her favorite spot), telling Him her sorrows.

Jesus was a celebrity, and He was God walking among them, but that did not stop Him from caring about Mary's pain. When Mary came to Jesus with her agony, He felt with her and for her: "When Jesus saw her weeping, and the Jews who had come along with her also weeping, he was deeply moved in spirit and troubled" (John 11:33).

He empathized with her pain so much—even though He knew it would soon go away when Lazarus was raised from the dead—that He wept (v. 35).

Think about that.

God met Mary in the darkest valley of her pain. He was there for her, not just in the good life experiences but in the most terrible incident she had ever lived through. The tears she saw Him cry were for her. Imagine seeing God cry in front of you in response to *your* pain. Would that change your relationship with Him?

Mary saw the God whose heart broke with hers, who cried with her, the God who was with her in every trial and trouble, the God who cared about her daily highs and lows and loved her in everything she did. That is what made the difference for Mary. That was the relationship that Mary was beginning to understand when Jesus showed up at Martha's house. God's incredible love for Mary empowered her to put aside every demand that life brought her—every single distraction—and spend time with the One who loved her so overwhelmingly.

YOUR RELATIONSHIP WITH GOD

Jesus was the one person who could show up at Martha's house and make Mary put aside all her stress, her tasks, and her worries, and drop everything to spend time with Him. What person would need to show up at your house to cause the same effect? Would it be a celebrity, a family member, a friend, your favorite singer or athlete, or some historical figure? I think if C. S. Lewis or Abraham Lincoln showed up at my doorstep, I would easily drop everything to spend every second I had listening to what they had to say.

So why do I not do the same thing with God? I literally have access to God's Word every second of my life, from the Bible on my shelf to the Bible app on my phone. I can pray anywhere I am. But I do not. God is at my door every second of my life, but I am too busy with life to sit at His feet and listen.

But Mary's story whispers to me what the problem might be. The reason I do not make time for God is because I forget who God is and what His relationship is with me. When I truly understand both of those things, it is impossible to stay away from time with Him.

So, let's unpack this: What is God's relationship with you and me? Here is a piece of reality for both of us: God was sitting up in heaven in all His power and glory, and He said, "It's great being God, but you know what would make it even better? Being able to share eternity with [insert your name here]." (Not a real quote from God.)

Yes, *you*.

God created this beautiful world full of wonderful and breathtaking places for you to live in and experience. He chose what century you would be born in, who your family would be, and what other people would exist during the same time as you. He beautifully orchestrated all these things for you.

Then, since He loves you so much, He didn't want to control whether you choose Him or not. He wanted you to have the free will to do what you want: follow Him or reject Him. Despite your sin, the One who has abundant love for you came to earth, experienced life how we experience it, lived perfectly, and died for you. He loves you that much! You are worth that sacrifice to Him. He did all that so when you screw up and do not follow Him perfectly, you still have the choice to be with Him forever. He has paid the price for your freedom. He has paid the price so that He can love you forever.

Imagine that. It's like having a friend that, no matter how horrible you are to them, even if you leave them for decades and hate them, they are still waiting with loving, open arms to welcome you back.

That is the God who loves you. That is the God you have the choice to ignore or spend time with each day. You can learn more about Him, be strengthened by Him, and let your life choices flow through the wisdom that He provides.

The more you do this, the more your love and peace will grow in Him. He will encourage you, strengthen you, prepare you, and be with you in every difficulty and joy of life. Does that sound like something you want?

An abundance of blessings come from spending time with God. I could write a whole book on that alone, but for today, answer the question for yourself. Do you want to make time with God a priority? Do you want to spend more time with the God whose tears fall down for you? The God who cares so deeply about you and every detail of your life?

If the answer is yes, let's figure out how we can make our precious quality time with God interwoven into our daily lives.

THE PLAN

Let's figure out the W^{2}HW, which is not a math problem or chemistry compound but the *where, when, how,* and *why* of spending time with God.

First, let's answer some easy questions.

Where Do You Want to Spend Time with God?

Thankfully, God is everywhere so He will kindly meet you wherever you want to go. Find a place where you feel comfortable and can unwind. It might be in nature with the sound of wind blowing through the trees, under the warm covers of your bed, in your favorite coffee shop with a delicious latte steaming next to you, on your morning drive when you can listen to audio, or just in a cozy cranny of your apartment. Find the place where you can clear your mind and will not constantly be distracted.

Pro-tip: Even if you do get distracted in this place by endless lists of things to do, keep a notebook by you so that every time your mind wants to remind you of something you need to do, you can write it down. Let the notebook remember instead of continuing to be distracted.

When Are You Going to Spend Time with God?

Commit right now to the amount of time you are going to set aside each day or each week. Start with something simple. Can you take away ten little minutes each day from something else? Think about it: what is going to bring you more joy? Netflix or Jesus? Scrolling social media or Jesus? Decide what amount of time works best for you.

After you decide how much time you'll spend with God, decide when you will spend it. First thing in the morning, when you get to work (with an emailed devotion), at night. Figure out what works best for your life.

Pro-tip: I have one of those cool sand-filled hourglasses that I like to use to get in a routine. This may seem a little too strict for you, so you definitely do not need to use my method, but when I do this, I am not counting the sand, waiting for my quality time to pass. I know that the timer represents the amount of time I have to push away everything else that wants to consume my time. This is God time, and I can deal with everything else when the sand all passes to the bottom.

How Are You Going to Spend Time with God?

After you choose where and when, decide what you are going to do in your quality time with God. What is piquing your interest right now? Do you want to study a modern-day issue in the context of the Bible? Do you have questions for God that you'd like to dig in to? Is there a topic or a book of the Bible that sounds interesting? Is there a devotional or book that you have been thinking about reading? Or do you want to spend time reflecting on the wonder of God in nature, singing praises to Him, praying, listening to worship music, writing poems, creating something, or listening to a podcast? The options are endless. Find what makes you excited. Sometimes going on a hike and marveling at God's creation fills me with wonder and awe for God. Sometimes the host of a podcast will make a profound point that wakes me up to a spiritual truth. Sometimes I cannot stop digging in to a portion of Scripture because it is exactly what I needed to hear. Sometimes I want to write my prayers down and journal with God. And sometimes I just want to listen to worship music to fill me up with His love.

It does not have to be the same thing every day, but choose some options that sound fun to you and make you look forward to spending time with God.

Super long pro-tip: There are many methods of studying the Bible. You can read and make art, write a song, journal, or whatever fits your personality. If you need a suggestion, I recommend the SOAP method. I was taught this acronym a few years ago, and it has been a game changer for me in reading the Bible, understanding it, and applying it to my life. It goes like this: Scripture, Observation, Application, and Prayer. Choose the part of the Bible you want to read and take one section (the contents under a heading, not necessarily a chapter) and do the following:

Step 1: Scripture

Pick one Bible verse or one idea from the portion of Scripture you read. Choose one thing that stands out to you from everything you read and write it down.

Step 2: Observation

Think about the context of the Scripture you chose. Answer questions like, What is going on in the world at that time? Who is speaking or being spoken to? What happened before and after this passage? Does it tie in to some other parts of the Bible, or is there another account of this in the Bible?

Not a biblical expert? No problem! One great way to get the context is to watch a YouTube video. I recommend The Bible Project, which has overviews and backgrounds for every book of the Bible.

Step 3: Application

Consider how this Scripture applies to your life. Jot down your answer in the context of your life today and your circumstances.

Step 4: Prayer

What does this piece of Scripture lead you to pray? Write out a prayer.

Growing up, I was a huge fan of the Inheritance Cycle series of books. Long story short, each dragon rider in these books had a telepathic connection with their dragon where they could talk to each other anytime and anywhere. I thought this was the coolest thing, and then one day I realized, I have that same connection with God. I can pray to Him anytime and anywhere, and He is even more powerful than an awesome dragon. Prayer is very powerful, so it is an important final step in our method.

There you go. One easy approach to reading the Bible. That is the method I use but find the special method or formula that works for you—whether it's journaling, creating art, writing a poem, or whatever your heart is called to do. I am sure that right now you have some inclination as to what that should be. Go follow it. Go enjoy it with God.

OK, last question.

Why Are You Going to Spend Time with God?

We have the when, we have the where, and we have the how, but why is the most important question. *Why* is the catalyst that will actually make quality time with God happen. *Why* is how we fight off the temptation of Satan and our own sinful nature that makes us too busy or makes us feel unmotivated to spend time with God.

Why? Let's get personal. Why should we spend time with God? We are not simply going through the motions of following a heartless ruler. God loves you with so much overwhelming love, and because of that He wants to be with you and spend time with you. He wants a relationship that is just as unique and beautiful as you are. Spending time with Him reminds us of all the good and important things in life.

PERSONALLY WRITTEN FOR YOU

Dietrich Bonhoeffer is one of the people I absolutely cannot wait to meet in heaven. This is not a book about him, so I will try to condense my praise (even though he fits into our theme as he was single most of his life). Dietrich was a pastor in Germany during World War II, and he took part in the assassination attempts on Hitler. (All it takes is that one sentence for me to think he is an insanely fascinating person, but I will move on.) With the events of World War II taking place in Germany, Dietrich saw how many of his fellow Germans were going to church but turning their backs to the Jews who needed their help. They did nothing to aid their suffering neighbors while the Nazis were coming up with everything from taking all Jewish references out of the Bible (which is hard because Jesus was Jewish) to replacing all crosses with swastikas.

One of the things Dietrich did was create a secret seminary to train people who wanted to become pastors. As part of his teaching, he had a very intense focus on reading the Bible. He made each student go to a quiet place on their own, read a portion of Scripture, and ask, How does this apply to me in my present circumstances?

One of his students said this:

> When you read the Bible, you must think that here and now God is speaking with me . . . [Bonhoeffer] wasn't as abstract as the Greek teachers and all the others. Rather, from the beginning, he taught us that we had to read the Bible as if it was directed at us, as the Word of God directly to us. Not something general, not something generally applicable, but rather with a personal relationship to us.[1]

A personal relationship to you.

Does that make you think of the Bible in a different way? You have a unique and personal relationship with God, and He had every word of the Bible written for a unique and personal relationship with you. Do you believe that? If so, it definitely changes the Bible-reading experience.

It means reading the story of Adam and knowing that some-day you will grab a cup of coffee with him in heaven and be able to ask, "Do you have a belly button?" It's reading the Bible with confidence that God has brought you to a certain portion of Scripture to speak to you in that very moment. What will

1. Eric Metaxas, *Bonhoeffer: Pastor, Martyr, Prophet, Spy* (Nashville: Thomas Nelson, 2010), 128–29.

you discuss today? What is He preparing you for? What will you learn?

My time with God has been a lifeline to me in my singleness. One time I was really struggling in deciding whether I should try to date someone or not. I just wanted a clear answer to know if I was wasting my time, hopes, and expectations, or if I should move on with my life and forget about them. I was stressing about it for weeks but after I prayed about all the feelings I was having, I started reading Ephesians. As I came across Ephesians 4:2 all the words on the page blurred out except two words: "be patient." My stomach plunged as I was filled with conviction. I was so worried about this tiny piece of my life that I let it overtake my trust in God. I let my worry make me forgot that God was working things out for my good, and the only thing I needed to do was trust Him.

That is the only time words have literally jumped off the pages of my Bible, but there have been so many times when I have been struggling with loneliness and then read a passage about God being with me or been upset about my singleness and then read a passage about His good and perfect plans.

In all my highs and lows of singleness, my time with God has been a source of renewal and comfort. It has been an anchor against the pressures of the world to conform and believe something is wrong with me. It has been something I can look forward to every day that reminds me that the most powerful being in the universe cares about me deeply.

Are you ready to spend time wrapped in God's love for you? Choose the thing that is the better use of your time. It will not be taken from you. As you continue to do this, you will feel the peace of being with God and the confidence in His plan for your life.

DIVING
DEEPER

1. What prevents you from spending quality time with God?
2. Do you feel guilty for not spending time with Him, or do you feel love pulling you to spend time with Him?
3. What are the benefits of spending time with God?
4. When it comes to spending time with God, how do you answer the questions where, when, how, and why?
5. How do you feel after you spend time with God?
6. Read Psalm 119:99, Psalm 119:105, and 2 Timothy 3:16–17 to see other blessings that come from spending quality time with God.

8

community

THE PACKAGE SAT on my front porch in all its glory: my new, luxurious memory foam mattress! As I looked at the box that had my purchase tightly wrapped inside, I remembered the first time I sat on one of these mattresses. I was a child in a furniture store with my parents. As my body sank into the comfort of the bed, I thought that someone had managed to fill a mattress with a cloud captured from the sky. I spent the whole time in the furniture store in awe of this comfortable bed, and I struggled to leave it behind when the shopping was over. From that day on, I decided that one day, when I grew up, I would sleep on one of those beds every night. Fifteen years later, my dream had come true.

But now, there was one problem that stood in the way of me sleeping on a cloud. The foam mattress was condensed into a heavy cylindrical package that was a little shorter than me, but it was much heavier than me. I lived alone, so somehow I had to lift this dense mattress up a flight of stairs and into my bedroom all by myself.

Am I blessed to have wonderful friends, family, and neighbors who will gladly help me in situations like this? Yes. Do I like to have to call these people and ask them for help? Absolutely not.

When it came to this heavy package sitting on my porch, my pride got the best of me, and I thought, *I'm a strong, independent woman, and I can do this on my own. I don't need to burden other people to help me.*

I put on my favorite workout clothes, played some pump-up music through my earbuds, and attempted to use physics and geometry (aka a lot of me shoving and grunting) to shift and roll the mattress up the stairs, into my bedroom, and onto my bedframe. I cut off the plastic surrounding the mattress to let it air out and expand into blissful comfort. I watched and smiled right as a sharp pain began to throb in my back. Apparently my body was not happy about the stress I had just put it through, and it was letting me know that I had made a horrible decision. As the spasms of pain in my back continued, I was at least thankful that I had a new mattress to lie on as I recovered for the rest of the day.

As I lay on my new cloud with an ice pack on my back, I was forced to think about my bad decision. Why did I always try to do things on my own, even when it could hurt me? I hated asking people for help, but why did I think trying to move a package that weighed more than I did was a good idea? I lay there in pain, digging into my pride, and I realized the truth I had been denying for so long: I hate to admit that I need other people. I hate to admit that I am incapable of doing something alone.

I CAN DO IT MYSELF

Do you ever feel pressure to prove your independence? To prove that you can take on the world all by yourself with no help from another man or woman? Maybe you see "successful" couples excelling in their careers, volunteering their time, gourmet cooking in their beautiful homes with crafted gifts, fancy cars, and self-sewn clothing, and you think, *I can do that on my own. I don't need a significant other to help me!* Then you go into "hyper-single mode," working hard and draining yourself to prove you can do just as much on your own as two people can do together.

For years, people have commented that my life would be easier if I had a husband to help me make food, take care of my house, keep track of bills, remember that it's recycling day, cook on the grill, and make my bed (overrated). A few months ago, I was at a store buying face wash. When the lady at the counter told me the number on the price tag, I replied, shocked, "Wow, that's expensive."

The lady responded, "Well, honey, maybe you can get your boyfriend to pay for it."

It took all my self-control not to yell that it is the twenty-first century and a woman does not need a boyfriend to buy face wash!

When people like the counter lady make me feel belittled in my single life, or incapable of doing as much as a couple can do, I feel a heavy push to prove to the world that I don't need anyone in order to thrive. I can take care of working full-time, managing a household, feeding myself, keeping my car running, unclogging my drains, keeping my plants alive, renovating my house, being the landlord of a duplex, and feeding my cat with no help from any other person.

This desire for complete independence makes it easy to push people away and not accept help. I feel like I am just a burden to them anyway. People have their own families, their own kids, their own problems, and even though they offer, do they really have time to help me? No, I feel it is better to rely only on myself.

But if I am being honest, the idea of a truly independent life is such a big fat lie. I do not grow my own food. I rely on others to do that and to deliver the food to grocery stores that other people run so that I can make food using recipes that other people created. I could not drive to work unless other people invented and built my car. I could not use a nice warm blanket unless other people raised adorable baby lambs, sheared their wool when they grew up, turned the wool into a blanket, and sold it to me.

For so long I have believed that true strength is being able to do everything on my own. In reality, it takes a lot more strength to ask people for help. It takes a lot more strength to admit how much help I truly need.

I have learned this lesson by accidentally hurting myself when not asking for help, like with my mattress, but I have also seen the impacts of acting like an island when it comes to my emotions. When I try to handle everything bothering me on my own, it becomes such a heavy weight to bear that it can overtake me with stress, anxiety, and panic attacks. It is amazing how light my burdens become when I am brave enough to share them with other people.

This is a lesson that I keep learning every day. We can definitely be strong and independent single people, but that does not mean that we should shut out people and their offers of help. God has placed a whole community of people in our lives so that we can both be a blessing to them and be blessed by them. As much as I have tried to deny it, community is an incredible gift, and it can give us some really amazing benefits when it comes to singleness. When people are deeply and truly loving us, it takes the pressure off to find a significant other to fill that void. When people help us with our burdens and tasks, it makes it easier to feel less desperate for that help from a boyfriend or girlfriend. Our next bachelorette, Mary Magdalene (aka "Magdalene" since there are way too many cool Marys in the Bible), really encompassed what it means to embrace the blessing of community. Let's take a look at her story to see how we can flourish with the people God has placed in our lives.

The Bachelorette:
MARY MAGDALENE

FRIENDS: Jesus, Mary, Mary, Mary
SKILLS: Supporting Jesus's ministry

Magdalene is such a fierce soldier in God's army. I cannot wait to get a breakfast burrito with her in heaven and just sit in awe of her the entire time. There are not a lot of passages on Magdalene, but every single time she is mentioned, it is in an amazing context. She helped support Jesus and His work financially (Luke 8:2-3), saw Jesus die (John 19:25), took care of His body when He died (Mark 16:1), and was the first person who Jesus appeared to after He rose from the dead (John 20:11-18). Can you imagine experiencing that moment in time! She was fully dedicated to God in her time, blessings, physical work, and spiritual work.

We don't have a ton of information on Magdalene's past, but we do know one very fascinating and terrifying detail about her life. Magdalene was possessed with not just one demon, or two demons, or three demons, or—OK, you get the point. She had seven demons possessing her at once (Luke 8:2)!

Now the Bible does not say why so many demons were in Magdalene, but I find it very fascinating because it fits so well into the theme of all the information we have on her. She was amazing at building and using her community, so I'm not surprised that it took an entire community of demons to possess her.

Every single time she is mentioned in the Bible after being freed from the demons, Magdalene is surrounded by a community of people. The first time we hear about her is a reference to her supporting Jesus's ministry.

After this, Jesus traveled about from one town and village to another, proclaiming the good news of the kingdom of God. The Twelve were with him, and also some women who had been cured of evil spirits and diseases: Mary (called Magdalene) from whom seven demons had come out; Joanna the wife of Chuza, the manager of Herod's household; Susanna; and many others. These women were helping to support them out of their own means. (Luke 8:1–3)

Here are a few examples where Magdalene is described as being with her crew of people:

- At Jesus's crucifixion and death (she was with Jesus's mother and His mother's sister, Mary the wife of Cleopas) (John 19:25)
- Anointing Jesus's body when He died (she was with Salome and Mary, the mother of James) (Mark 16:1)
- On the way to the tomb after Jesus's death, only to be surprised with His resurrection (she was with "the other Mary") (Matt. 28:1–10)

These examples teach us that Mary must have been a very popular baby name when all these people were born!

The cool thing about Magdalene's community is that they were there to support one another emotionally. Together they went through what must have been the most emotionally devastating event that ever happened on earth: Jesus dying on the cross after bearing the sins of the world. Thankfully, they also experienced never-ending joy and happiness when Jesus rose from the dead.

Community is an extremely significant tool in our Christian arsenal. Community can support us when we go on the umpteenth bad date. Community can encourage us when we are angry and upset about our single lives. Community can be there to care about the highs and lows of each day. Community can help guide us in the truth and love of God. Community can remind us that we are not fighting alone. Magdalene's life is not the only place where community is mentioned in the Bible. Here are a few other examples:

As iron sharpens iron, so one person sharpens another. (Prov. 27:17)

So that there should be no division in the body, but that its parts should have equal concern for each other. If one part suffers, every part suffers with it; if one part is honored, every part rejoices with it. Now you are the body of Christ, and each one of you is a part of it. (1 Cor. 12:25-27)

And let us consider how we may spur one another on toward love and good deeds, not giving up meeting together, as some are in the habit of doing, but encouraging one another—and all the more as you see the Day approaching. (Heb. 10:24-25)

God has given us community, just like Magdalene, to sharpen us, encourage us, and help us live life together. Magdalene was able to experience that in her time with Jesus, and we can experience it in our lives as well. As single people, we do not need to live our lives alone. We do not need a significant other to see that God has provided so many people to support us and help us enjoy and persevere in the life He has given to us.

YOUR COMMUNITY

What does your community look like right now? Who are the people you surround yourself with? Is your community a picture of what the Bible describes, people sharpening and supporting each other? Do you feel like you have people to emotionally support you? Do you have people who can build you up in your single life? Do you have people you can admit your sins and insecurities to? Do they encourage and support you in your beliefs and dreams?

Or when you think of the people around you, do you feel drained and discouraged? Are you sick of arguments that go nowhere, time spent with people who talk about only themselves, people who are negative Nancys or bad influences, people who don't really understand who you are or use passive-aggressive actions and judgments to make you feel small?

I never used to think of my community intentionally. I thought it was something that just happened—which definitely can be the case—but then I started college and struggled living with no real community. I went to an engineering college full of guys who loved to play video games mixed with the occasional evening of LARPing (Live Action Role Playing—think fake swords and battles). Since most of them did not leave their rooms often, it took me a lot of time to find my crew of people who I could be real, open, and raw with. Those early years of college where I did not have a good community really taught me how important God made community. I missed sharing my feelings, I missed bonding with other people, and I missed laughing so hard that tears rolled down my face.

So how do we experience community that can fill us up and encourage us and also provide a space we can pour our time and talents into? Maybe God has already blessed you with this group of people, but you wish that you could make some changes. Maybe you long to be surrounded by people who understand the depths of your soul. If so, we can work on this together. We can work on how to balance all the relationships in our lives, whether they are lifetime friends, exes, our mail carrier, family members, or the guy you always see on the bike trail. And we can do it by thinking about a bridge.

BRIDGE

Picture the biggest bridge you've ever seen in your life—I'm imagining one that goes over a giant body of water and makes me terrified to drive across it. When storms come, the wind and waves press against the foundational pillars holding the bridge up, and since they stand strong, cars continue to pass back and forth in safety (despite the emotional terror of some of the drivers).

Now picture your community as a bridge. There are three main parts: the foundational pillars that hold everything up, the actual road that the cars drive on, and the cars that pass from one end to the other.

In this metaphor, you are the road. You are held up by pillars, and you are the means by which cars pass from one point to another. The people in your life are the cars and the pillars, but it is very important to know who is who.

Cars travel over bridges at some point in time, just as people share time with you at some point in their life journey. Sometimes they spend a long time on your bridge, stopping at a scenic overlook or driving slowly to take in the sights. These people could be friends, family members, coworkers, people in your classes, your roommate, neighbors, or anyone else in your life. Other times, cars zip by so fast you can barely believe they were even there, like the cashier at the grocery store or the receptionist at your doctor's office. The majority of people in your life are cars.

Then there are the pillars. These are the people who truly know and understand you, who you can go to in the hardest of times. They fill up your emotional bucket when you feel completely drained. They can be honest with you, even when it hurts. These are the hobbits traveling with Frodo in *Lord of the Rings*, Dory to Marlin in *Finding Nemo*, Ron and Hermione to Harry Potter— whoever keeps you going when life gets difficult.

When you think of a bridge, you know how important the pillars are. They must be strong, because if they crumble, the whole bridge will fall, taking you and the cars with you down. Does that seem extreme? Think about bad days you have had. I have had extremely frustrating days at work that were full of meetings that could have been emails and people who did not seem to want to do their jobs. I work with many great people, but it is very important for me to know who my pillars are and who are simply cars passing by. When I'm frustrated and go to a pillar, like my mentor, I am encouraged and built up so that I can remain positive toward my team. If, on the other hand, I treat a car as a pillar, I may enter into a depressing conversation with someone where I just complain and get more depressed. Then when I work with my team, I bring that anger and frustration with me. Consider a negative person in your life. Does it ever feel like a cloud comes on you when you spend time with them? Maybe you are allowing them to be a pillar when they are really a car.

There will be many people in your life. God made us all unique and chose to have you born in a certain time period with certain people in a certain place. Don't feel guilty about categorizing the people in your life as pillars and cars. Even Jesus had his inner circle. You are not thinking anything bad about a person by acknowledging that they are a car; you are just being honest with yourself about how God created you and your mind to work. If you make someone a pillar—if you put your emotional trust and support in them—and they do not hold you up, then the consequences are much more catastrophic than if you consider them as a car in your life. I would encourage you to make the pillars in your life strong Christians. They are the ones who can encourage you in God's Word and help you remember how much He loves you.

It's OK if your pillars change frequently. In the same way, you are going to be a pillar for different people at different times. No one is perfect and no one can be a perfect friend, so when you see a crack in one of your pillars, make sure you go and hold their bridge up and be strong for them.

If you are trying to figure out who your pillars are or should be, I encourage you to make a list of what you want and do not want in a pillar. You get to be picky here, but spoiler alert, you do not get to be picky with cars. Think of the people in your life and see what characteristics stand out as good characteristics of a support system. Here's my list:

Want: Christian, good listener, empathetic, caring, honest, raw, positive

Don't Want: Always on cell phone, fake, tends to gossip, bad listener, complains a lot

Think of your wants and don't wants, then make a list of the people who embody the good characteristics on your pillar list.

- _____

- _____

- _____

How does your list look? Are you letting these people be pillars in your life? When you feel overwhelmed, broken, angry, or upset about being single, can you be raw and open with these people? Here are some other questions you might want to ask:

- Does this person drain or fill up my emotional bucket?
- Will this person guide me in the way God wants me to go?
- Does this person give me advice as to what is best for me, instead of what's best for them? Will they try to talk me into something because they will get something out of it?

If you feel like you don't have enough of the right pillars in your life, there are a couple of things you can do.

- *Pray.* Ask God to put the right people in your life so you can best serve Him.
- *Leverage your existing connections.* Are there people in your life you can invest more in—people you can spend more time with and get to know who can maybe become pillars? Take the leap, be open, and share something vulnerable with them. I once shared my life story with a coworker as we rode the train together. She shared hers back, and we became deep friends from that moment on.
- *Seek out pillars in the right places.* Join a Bible study or go to church events. Sorry, you are not going to find your pillars at a concert where the artists cannot stop speaking horrible things. Go to the places and events that the type of people you are looking for will be. Also, consider actively seeking out a mentor. Find someone who has a life, a faith, a career, a business, or a hobby that you admire. Ask them if they would be willing to mentor you. Nine times out of ten, if the person has time, they will be thrilled to share their growth and passion with you so you can grow as well.
- *Find people through shared interests.* Maybe you've moved somewhere and the closest church is full of people who are your grandparents' age. They are nice, but they might not understand everything you are going through. Or maybe there are a lot of Christians around you, but your personalities don't match so you're uncomfortable being completely raw with them. If you fall into either of these scenarios, I suggest a method that's a little harder, but it's one I have used to find pillars—through shared hobbies. Join a sports league, a rock climbing group, or a group for

computer programming enthusiasts—whatever lines up with your hobbies. Meetup is a great way to find people in your area with similar interests (www.meetup.com). There are even friend-meeting apps like Bumble (it has a setting for finding friends). Or consider finding people through professional organizations that are great for meeting new people. As you start making connections and sharing your values in these groups, it will become easier to find like-minded people.

Once you establish a good group of pillars, you can better serve the cars in your community by giving them a beautiful road to travel on.

CORRIE TEN BOOM

Corrie ten Boom is one of my favorite examples of doing this. Her bridge traveled through one of the darkest times in history: the Holocaust. Corrie ten Boom is another phenomenal single warrior in the history books. She was single her whole life and lived in the Netherlands during World War II.

When the Germans took over her country, Corrie and her family became leaders in the underground movement who helped hide and save Jews by leading those around them to fight for what was right. At first, Corrie was able to keep up with helping the Jews who came to her door—getting them an address of a place to stay or getting them ration cards so they could have food—but then it became much more overwhelming. She realized she needed more pillars to help safely move the cars on her road, and she trusted God to help provide them. She said,

> But still the hunted people kept coming, and the needs were often more complicated than rations cards and addresses. If a Jewish woman became pregnant, where could she go to have her baby?

If a Jew in hiding died, how could he be buried? . . . An uncanny realization had been growing in me. We were friends with half of Haarlem! We knew nurses in the maternity hospital. We knew clerks in the Records Office. We knew someone in every business and service in the city. We didn't know, of course, the political views of all the people. But—and here I felt a strange leaping of my heart—God did![1]

Corrie's phenomenal community did not stop there. She was imprisoned with her sister, Betsie—one of her pillars—and in every cell and barrack the sisters were imprisoned in, they were able to create a prospering community. They would read their smuggled Bible each night, and women from all over the world would gather in close to listen. In one concentration camp, they had to have two Bible studies because so many people wanted to partake in the experience each night.

After Corrie was released, she traveled the world to talk about the joy in the darkness. She went on to create a place for survivors of World War II to recover (including places for the Germans who had hurt her), then she said this: "Every experience God gives us, every person He puts in our lives is the perfect preparation for the future that only He can see."[2]

Look at the journey Corrie's cars had when they came into her life. She, along with her pillars, safely guided them from one point to another. It is estimated that Corrie and her family saved more than eight hundred people with their underground workers, and that doesn't even take into account all the work she did after the war to help people emotionally and spiritually.

Corrie knew who her pillars were. She knew the people who were fighting in the battle with her and knew who she could

1. Corrie ten Boom, John Sherrill, and Elizabeth Sherrill, *The Hiding Place* (Uhrichsville, OH: Barbour Publishing, 1971), 85–86.
2. Corrie ten Boom, John Sherrill, and Elizabeth Sherrill, *The Hiding Place* (New York: Bantam Books, 1974), viii.

trust and rely on. This allowed her to help so many more people than she would have been able to help on her own. We will talk more about serving your cars in chapter 10, but for now, pay attention to your pillars. And with your pillars, give your cars the best journey they can have as they interact with you, just like Corrie did. You might not know why certain people cross your path on this side of death, but you can always be a light to them, and you may be surprised by the beautiful results.

DIVING
DEEPER

1. Why has God given us community?
2. Consider a time when you felt supported by your community. Consider a time when you didn't.
3. What are important traits and characteristics you'd like your pillars to have?
4. Who are some of the pillars in your life?
5. Are you making any cars into pillars? What is the impact?
6. Are you happy with the number of pillars in your life? If not, how will you find more?
7. How can you provide a beautiful journey for the cars on your bridge?

9

purpose

WHEN IS THE LAST TIME you really paid attention to the dreams that swirl around in your head? Yes, I know there is the dream of being with someone and living happily ever after, but if you gently nudge that dream to the side, what else comes to the surface?

I remember seeing an inspiring banner at a cheerleading competition in high school. It read SHOOT FOR THE MOON. EVEN IF YOU MISS, YOU'LL LAND AMONG THE STARS.

I immediately cringed and thought, *No. If you miss, you'll end up floating in space until you run out of air and die all alone in cold, deep space. Maybe you would land among the stars eventually, but you wouldn't be alive to know. That sounds terrible!*

As you can imagine from hearing just one snippet of my high school mindset, I've always had a pretty Scrooge-like view on pursuing my dreams.

As the end of high school was creeping up and all my classmates and I had to somehow decide what our future career paths would be, I did not think, *What type of work will make me excited to wake up each day?* or *What career will I find fulfilling?* Instead, I stomped on any dreams that may have been growing inside me in order to take a path toward something I was good at and, more importantly, would lead to a secure job with good pay. Sure, I had dreams, but I could not see how they would do me any good. They were just a distraction to me pursuing a stable career.

I used to think that dreams were only for long meetings and boring lectures: a great way to pass the time, but not practical for real life. Yes, I loved to mentally design my dream home that included a lazy river moat, treehouses, secret tunnels, horses, and a giant hidden library. I loved to write stories and poems. I had many things I was bad at but still enjoyed. But why pay attention to those things when I could work hard and have a successful career? Why try to pursue those things when they could be unstable, lead to insecurity, expose my weaknesses, or make my life uncomfortable?

Whenever I had a dream, I politely smiled at it and waved it away as soon as it appeared. No matter how many times it came knocking on my door. No matter how bored, unfulfilled, and unhappy I felt. But thankfully, everything changed a few years ago in Madison, Wisconsin.

My friend Anna invited me to a Jon Foreman concert (aka the lead singer of the band Switchfoot). As we drove to the venue, we were confused by the rather unconventional information on our concert tickets. They read: "Movie at 7. Concert at 8."

"Movie?" we both questioned. We wondered if the concert tickets had a mistake on them. After grabbing dinner, we arrived in time to see the mysterious movie and, wow, what an experience!

Jon Foreman played his documentary *25in24*. It followed Jon as he pursued a dream God had placed on his heart: playing twenty-five concerts in twenty-four hours.

When Jon first shared this dream, everyone thought he was biting off more than he could chew, but they still agreed to make it happen. The day of twenty-five concerts came and Jon traveled across California with different musicians and performed at different venues. He played with the high school band at his alma mater, at the children's hospital where his daughter was cared for, with his mom on a massive pipe organ, and even with a mariachi band at his favorite Mexican restaurant.

The journey featured car issues and sleep deprivation, but as the hours ticked by, Jon was able to fill growing crowds of people with joy, inspiration, and hope.

At the start of the concert, we were each handed a piece of paper with the words "My dream is ___" printed on it. My heart pounded as I knew what needed to fill the blank space. A whisper in my mind was slowly growing louder and louder that I needed to write a book on singleness based off of my experiences and faith. A book that would encourage and uplift anyone who was struggling with their single status in life.

My heart was pounding through the rest of the concert. It was a magical evening where we could write song requests on pieces of paper, then Jon would read them and play them. One woman said her dream was to sing with Jon. He read it and brought her onstage for a beautiful duet.

After the concert, I went home and looked at my piece of paper with a line in my head from a song Jon had sung: "What happens next? I dare you to move."[1]

I looked at the piece of paper and was hit with a realization. Maybe what I had been telling myself for so many years was a lie. Maybe dreams were not a distraction from our duty and purpose. Maybe dreams were something God gives us as a unique and beautiful way to serve Him—handcrafted for each of us by

1. Switchfoot, "Dare You to Move," *The Beautiful Letdown*, Sony BMG Music Entertainment, 2003, compact disc.

our perfect and loving Creator. And maybe God truly does want us to follow those dreams.

I looked at the paper and knew I needed to do it. The dream that had always been pushing on me, constantly coming up in my mind, needed to stop being ignored. I finally decided I was going to write my book. If you are reading this, you know that dream came true.

WHAT ARE YOUR DREAMS?

What about you? Have you listened to the dreams that dance through your mind? Not the dreams at night of flying on dragons, catching robbers, eating a hundred donuts in one sitting, and learning to breathe underwater so you can swim with dolphins and tropical fish. No, I'm talking about the little voice in your mind that whispers to you about a life that makes you excited. The whisper of a project, a career, a talent, a song, a goal, a craft, a volunteer opportunity, an organization, a business, a platform, a story, a way to love the people around you, or some other dream that has been patiently waiting for you to pay attention to it. Maybe you are thinking of something right now—your bakery, your ministry, your art—but your dream seems intimidating, and you feel so unqualified to start it that you are scared to try to pursue it. Or maybe it seems like something simple or unimportant—helping your neighbor or calling your friend—and you think your dream is too little to care about. Or maybe you are sick of your monotonous life but you are praying and asking God to give you that dream to take your life from gray to color. You want something to chase and pursue, but you are not sure what it should be.

No matter where you are in knowing or recognizing those dreams, it is important to start paying attention to the little voices and feelings that are nudging you. Even if they seem inconvenient or might not exactly make sense yet. One of the blessings of being single is that we have this unique opportunity to follow our dreams without the constraint of a relationship. (Unless you are a single parent, in which case, keep rocking it—you are keeping your children alive, and you are amazing!) Sure, we have plenty of work and responsibilities that we have to stay on top of, but we also have the flexibility to use our free time exactly how we want to use it. I can stay up into the late hours of the night and write, knowing I do not have a significant other who will be impacted by my grumpy mood from lack of sleep. If I have airline points, I can buy a plane ticket today, hop on a plane, and visit a friend in another state without having to consult someone else's schedule. Since I am single, I can use all the time that would be poured into a relationship—phone calls, dates, and long conversations—and use it to find, explore, and pursue the dreams on my heart that make me feel alive.

If you choose to use your time to discover and follow your dreams, I guarantee you are going to start enjoying your life more than you could ever imagine. Instead of focusing on your singleness, you will come alive with the rush of figuring out and becoming the person that God created you to be. You will stop focusing on your problems and remember the much bigger picture that is way beyond you and your little world. If your dream is to save puppies and you are surrounded by adorable puppies each day, that is going to be a great and healthy experience for your brain that will take your mind off of being single. If your dream is to make the best donuts in town, think of how much joy you will experience when people's faces show how happy they are after taking one bite of your creation. If your dream is to help teenagers in your community, who knows how much that will grow you and how God will use that for His good. The possibilities of your life are endless. Are you ready to explore them?

Our next bachelor is a great inspiration for showing what can happen when we follow the dreams God has placed on our hearts. He goes through the hardships and the joys of the entire process.

Let's take a look at our next bachelor, Nehemiah, to see what can happen when we choose to follow our dreams.

> *The Bachelor:*
> ## NEHEMIAH
>
> PROFESSION: Cupbearer
> FAMILY: Son of Hakaliah
> GOALS: Rebuilding Jerusalem

Nehemiah was a cupbearer to the Persian king Artaxerxes (feel free to share that baby name with any friends who are pregnant). Nehemiah was living during a time when the Persians had conquered the Babylonians who had conquered his people, the Israelites. Early on in Nehemiah's story, we notice some rather odd behavior. Nehemiah is told that his people's city, Jerusalem, was broken down and the gates had been burned by fire. His reaction is this: "When I heard these things, I sat down and wept. For some days I mourned and fasted and prayed before the God of heaven" (Neh. 1:4).

Yes, the destruction of the city of Jerusalem was sad, especially since Jerusalem represented to the Israelites that God was with His people. But the weird piece of this story is that the city had been destroyed 140 years before Nehemiah wept for it. Nehemiah did not follow Jerusalem on Twitter or Facebook to get constant updates, but news in that day did not take 140 years to travel either. Nehemiah already knew Jerusalem had been destroyed, and in this one particular instance in his life, he was extremely convicted by the destruction. He mourned and fasted for days. He wanted something to be done to restore Jerusalem. He later described this desire as "what my God had put in my heart to do for Jerusalem" (2:12). With this, Nehemiah took the first step in following a dream.

Step 1: Identify the Dream

How did Nehemiah go about following this dream to restore Jerusalem? The very first thing he did was pray to God and ask for help and success in his endeavor.

Step 2: Pray

Then Nehemiah worked with the people around him to pursue this dream. As Nehemiah mourned Jerusalem, his sorrow was noted by King Artaxerxes. When the king inquired about it, God granted Nehemiah favor with the ruler. So much so that King Artaxerxes not only let Nehemiah leave his job to rebuild Jerusalem but also sent an army of officers and cavalry with him so Nehemiah would arrive safely and gave him letters so he could get timber to build the city.

After arriving in Jerusalem with his fancy escort, Nehemiah rode around the whole city to assess the damage and work he needed to do. I can imagine that seeing the destruction of the city had to be somewhat intimidating since much work was needed to rebuild it. But Nehemiah rallied the people around him to help. There are thirty-two verses of details of all the people who helped restore Jerusalem. There is no way Nehemiah could have done it on his own, but God provided the right people at the right time to fulfill his dream.

Step 3: Assemble the Team

Just because God placed this dream on Nehemiah's heart did not mean that it would be all smooth sailing. Nehemiah faced plenty of challenges and headaches in pursuing the success of his dream, which brings us to the next chunk of steps.

Steps 4–20: Persevere

During the rebuilding process, two villains kept coming in to sabotage Nehemiah. Their names were Sanballat the Horonite and Tobiah the Ammonite official (what a mouthful). We will call them "San" and "Toby." San and Toby were mad that anyone was supporting the Israelites or supporting anything to do with Israel, so they did everything they could to stop the work on Jerusalem. They started by mocking Nehemiah and his plans. When that didn't work, they got their A-team together (including the Arabs, the Ammonites, and the men of Ashdod) and conspired to kill the builders.

Nehemiah then had half of the men work while the other half held weapons to guard the people. The Bible even says, "Those who carried materials did their work with one hand and held a weapon in the other" (4:17).

Can you even imagine this? Have you ever done any home renovations? They are hard enough when done normally. Next time you paint your walls, think about rolling the paint with one hand while holding a sword in your other hand. Imagine the dedication of the people working on these repairs!

The challenges did not stop with external people. The headaches only grew worse when Nehemiah's own Jewish leaders started taxing his workers so hard that people were sold into slavery to pay their debts. Nehemiah put out this fire, and then San and Toby came back to lure him out of the city. They even hired false prophets to intimidate him.

Despite all the attacks, Nehemiah did not give up. After only fifty-two days, the walls of Jerusalem were rebuilt. If only road construction in Wisconsin could go that fast!

Step 21: Praise God

After the success in Jerusalem, thousands of Israelites returned to celebrate and dedicated their lives to God. This all went back to a dream God placed on one man's heart, a dream that seemed impossible since the man was completely unqualified to fulfill it. But Nehemiah took that dream and followed it. The joy of the

Lord revitalized and pushed him in his endeavor, and look at how God blessed the outcome of that dream was!

YOUR DREAMS

If God can use a cupbearer to rebuild a city, imagine how He can use you. Has God put anything on your heart like He did for Nehemiah?

If nothing is coming to mind, a helpful question to ask yourself is "What breaks my heart?" Think about what things in the world make you upset or angry. Maybe it is human trafficking, homelessness, bullying, or some other cause. Maybe it is someone in your life who is suffering. Is there something on your heart that can make the world a better place? That can help spread God's love or make this world a little more beautiful?

In college, I had one of those instances of something breaking my heart (beyond breaking off an engagement). I was representing my campus ministry at a fair that students could come to in order to learn about the activities on our campus. I talked to many students throughout the night, and at one point a cute foreign exchange student came up to me and started asking about campus ministry. In his German accent, he asked me where I went to church, and then a few days later (guys, pay attention, this was very impressive!) he showed up at my church at the service I attended.

We started hanging out more, playing board games and getting drinks after school, and it did not take us too long to get into some deep conversations. Despite his meeting me at a campus ministry booth, going to church, and continuing to go to campus ministry with me, he was a hard-core atheist. Young, naive Hannah thought, *Challenge accepted*. We had two weeks before he went back to his home in Germany, so I poured tons of time and research into unraveling his reasons for not being a Christian.

At one point, he told me the heart of it all. He used to be a Christian, but he had dated a girl and when they broke up, he was absolutely devastated. He had pleaded with God, "God, if You are real and care, do something about this. Get us back together." But despite praying this prayer over and over, God answered him with a no. As a result, my new friend was convinced that God could not exist. And sadly, it did not end there. One of the last nights before he had to fly home, he told me he was so devastated by his breakup that he had planned to end his life (thankfully he did not follow through).

My heart was broken. Broken for him and for his situation. Broken for all the people who have gone through singleness feeling like God does not care about them. Broken for all the people who have decided to give up on God because they cannot understand how He can be good and real and let them go through an awful breakup.

But the stories did not stop with my friend from Germany. After years of conversations with friends in heartbreaking and frustrating dating (and lack-of-dating) situations, my heart was so burdened that I needed to do something. It did not hit me instantly; it was a combination of years of things happening that finally led to the moment in Madison, at the Jon Foreman concert, when I realized I needed to do something about the thing that broke my heart. I needed to fight for people who feel alone and abandoned in their singleness.

Is anything weighing on you like it did for me and Nehemiah? Something that makes you want to change the world? It doesn't have to be massive: every single thing is important. It might be helping a friend with a problem they are going through or giving basic necessities to a person experiencing homelessness. It could be helping the environment, or animals, or kids, or the elderly, or making great food to bring people joy. It could be creating art or starting a business that has been on your mind for a long time. Every time you feel the need to do something, write it down, then see if there is a pattern. See if you can identify the dream, our first step from Nehemiah's path to pursuing dreams.

Step 1: Identify the Dream

You might have something in your mind as you read through this, even if it is just a small whisper. If you are still struggling to come up with anything, spend some time in prayer. You are wonderfully and specially made. God has plans in store for you. He may not show you them right now, but pray for patience and pray for guidance.

If you have a glimpse of a dream, a full design of a new business, or anything in between, we can move to Nehemiah's next step.

Step 2: Pray

Does your dream scare you or overwhelm you at all? If I am being honest, my dreams often terrify me. I feel like I am not capable of making a difference. Even if I try, I am just one person. What can I really accomplish? That is why it is so important to bring your dream to God. To be open, honest, and raw with Him. To ask whether you should move forward and then ask for His blessing and guidance if you do. The God who loves you and died for you is listening to you. Use that blessing to help guide you in your dream.

Step 3: Assemble the Team

You have the dream and you prayed about it, but now where do you even begin? Maybe as you analyze what it will take to pursue your dream—like Nehemiah riding around broken-down Jerusalem—you will start to realize that you might not be able to do everything alone. There might be gaps in your skills or knowledge, or maybe you simply need people to encourage you. The beautiful truth is that God has provided people to help you, as we discussed in chapter 8. Nehemiah used his community well. He had the help of the king of Persia, along with tons of Israelites, to rebuild Jerusalem. He did not make his dream happen on his own; God provided a whole team to help make it happen.

If you start to think about how to pursue your dream, you might be surprised about the system of support and experts that God has provided for you. As I started to pursue my dream of writing a book, I was blown away by the number of people already in my life that were there to help me. I knew people who had written books before, people who knew how to do graphic design and photography for social media, people who could design my website, people to pray for me and be my cheerleaders, people who could spell, and people who could fill so many of the gaps that I could not fill entirely on my own. God has placed the right people at the right time in my life for me to follow my dream, and He can do the exact same thing for you. Think about the parts of your dream where you can work with someone else or leverage an organization that exists already. Think of who can help you in the areas where you have gaps. It might simply be someone to encourage you, but you do not have to do this alone!

Steps 4–20: Persevere

Just because God gives you a dream, it does not mean that He is going to make it as easy a path as floating down a lazy river. God gave Nehemiah his dream, and look at the incredible opposition he faced—ridicule, death threats, construction while holding weapons, his own people making life difficult, and so much more. People might make fun of you. They may say you will never succeed, or they may try to stop you. You may feel incapable. You may be overcome with fear or incredible doubt. But if you are following what God has placed on your heart, you need to push through those trials, keep asking God to help you through them, and trust Him to be with you in it all. The fight is not yours alone. It's God's as well.

Let the joy of the Lord be your strength to persevere.

You have God's love, His eternal salvation, and His support. He can help you through any challenge you face, whether it comes from other people or your own mind.

Step 21: Praise God

Take a step back and look at what God has used you for! A dream may not go where you intended it to. Maybe you will grow on the way to the outcome. Maybe people will be blessed in a way you did not expect. No matter what happens, be sure to thank God for blessing you with your talents and inclinations to follow your dreams.

That's it! Twenty-one steps to accomplishing the dreams God placed on your heart. Are you ready to start following your dreams? I pray God makes them clear and gives you the strength to boldly follow them. I cannot wait to see where they go!

I want to give you one last piece of inspiration before you close the pages of this chapter and hopefully start spending some time pursuing your dreams. In an interview on Mike Donehey's *Chasing the Beauty* podcast, Gareth Gilkeson of the Irish Christian band Rend Collective was asked for advice on following dreams. Gareth responded, "Remember that you are God's dream."[2]

Think about that. At some point (or maybe always), God had the dream of creating this world and all the people in it. God had the dream of experiencing existence with you. To be with you in your highs and lows. To be with you in chasing your dreams. And to be with you in heaven forever. Being with you was a dream God had, and He made it come true. You existing is God's dream.

That is such a helpful reminder to relieve myself from the pressure of scrambling and striving to "achieve" dreams. Of despairing when they get hard. Of getting frustrated if they do not work out how I imagine. You and me existing and being ourselves

2. Mike Donehey, "Episode 13: Coming to America," November 4, 2021, in *Chasing the Beauty*, produced by AccessMore, https://www.accessmore.com/episode/Ep-13-Coming-To-America. Transcribed by the author.

is what God wanted. We are His dream. That realization can give me strength to accomplish any endeavor in my life. I hope it is a great reminder of who you are and who is with you as you step out and pursue the dreams God has placed on your heart.

DIVING DEEPER

1. Has God placed any dreams on your heart that you feel you should pursue?
2. What keeps you from pursuing your dreams?
3. What breaks your heart in this world?
4. Have you previously followed a dream? What happened?
5. What is the next step you need to take in following a dream?
6. What helps you persevere when you face obstacles?
7. What does it mean to you that you are God's dream?

10

serving

WHO IS YOUR FAVORITE SUPERHERO? Is it Batman, Wonder Woman, Iron Man, Black Widow, or Thor? Or do you prefer more obscure ones that apparently exist, like Squirrel Girl, Doorman, Arm-Fall-Off Boy (he does exactly what you expect from the name), or Fruit Boy? Or do you have some other character—real or fictional—who inspires you, like Sherlock Holmes, Martin Luther King Jr., Frodo Baggins, the woman who put the tent peg in that guy's head in Judges 4:12, James Bond, Madame Currie, Robin Hood, or Pocahontas?

Our movies, TV shows, and books are filled with these types of heroes who use their miraculous powers, singing prowess, magic, brainpower, courage, good looks, and technology to save the world in a matter of a few hundred pages of a book or a few hours of a movie. It seems like every single month, I can grab a bowl of popcorn, lounge in a comfy chair, and watch how a superhuman saves the entire world from a huge catastrophe.

I love the adventure, the stories of good overcoming evil, and the inspiration I get to save the world when I consume these stories, but there is also a rather dark side effect that happens to me.

After the film is over, the TV show is done, or the last page of the book is read, thoughts creep into my mind, reminding me of my inadequacies. These thoughts push me to compare myself to these heroes. It does not take long for me to feel like my life is incredibly boring and that I cannot make an impact on the world. I want to help millions of people, but I was not involved in some freak accident that gave me the powers of a cat, sloth, or some other animal. I am not a genius or a clever billionaire—I don't even feel qualified to do the job I am paid for while surrounded by people who are smarter and more experienced than me. There are so many people who are wiser, funnier, better looking, more creative, and more talented than me. How can little me possibly make a difference in this giant world?

In the last chapter, we explored how to live out the dreams God has placed on our hearts. We focused on personal projects and the fulfillment that we can have by utilizing the talents God has given us. Those dreams we explored could take days, weeks, months, years, or even decades of growth. Those are something that will hopefully continue to grow and evolve as you chase them throughout your life. Today, I want to explore something that is not so long-term. I want to explore what you and I have right now: not the future, not the past, but this very moment that we are experiencing. God has given us the power to change the world right now, and as I have dug into this truth, I've been surprised by what that actually looks like. It is not impressive fighting skills to win battles, overcoming dark magic by singing and dancing, or going on a dangerous and toll-taking quest to defeat evil. *Right now we have the power to do something that can truly make a difference in the world—let our light shine.*

It seems so simple. It seems hard to believe. Let's take a look at how this plays out by looking at our next two bachelorettes: Naomi and Ruth.

The Bachelorettes:
NAOMI and RUTH

Naomi

HOMETOWN: Bethlehem

NICKNAME: Mara

Ruth

NATIONALITY: Moabite

SKILLS: Loyalty

First, let's jump into Naomi's life.

Naomi was a wife and mother of two sons. They lived in the town of Bethlehem, but a great famine overtook the land, so they moved to Moab (where they were foreigners outside the land of Israel), hoping for a better life. Then tragedy struck. Naomi's husband died, and then both of Naomi's sons died as well. She was left as a widow in a foreign land, and her entire family was gone.

I don't think it takes a lot of imagination to realize how tragic this was and how heartbroken Naomi must have felt after losing her husband and sons. Her grief was so great that she said, "The Lord's hand has turned against me!" (Ruth 1:13). She even asked people to start calling her Mara, saying, "The Almighty has made my life very bitter. I went away full, but the Lord has brought me back empty. Why call me Naomi?" (vv. 20–21).

In her sorrow, Naomi heard that God was helping her people back home in Israel. With nothing to keep her in Moab, she decided to journey back home. Before her sons had died, they had married Moabite women named Orpah and Ruth, who were now grieving widows. Naomi told her daughters-in-law that she was going to her homeland, but she encouraged them to stay behind.

They could find new husbands in Moab, and if they went with Naomi, she had nothing to offer them. Orpah listened and tearfully parted with Naomi, but Ruth persisted in staying with her mother-in-law. Ruth said,

> Don't urge me to leave you or to turn back from you. Where you go I will go, and where you stay I will stay. Your people will be my people and your God my God. Where you die I will die, and there I will be buried. May the LORD deal with me, be it ever so severely, if even death separates you and me. (vv. 16–17)

What an incredible declaration! Both Naomi and Ruth were facing the grief of losing loved ones. Naomi was consumed in her grief, but Ruth decided to still be a light to Naomi in this dark time. Ruth chose to leave the land and people she knew in order to be a blessing to her mother-in-law. She put aside her own best interests to shine light on the person whom God placed right in front of her.

After they returned to Israel, Ruth went to gather food for Naomi, ended up marrying the guy whose field she was gathering from, and had a baby. Through Ruth, Naomi's life took a drastic turn toward happiness. People even said to Naomi,

> Praise be to the LORD, who this day has not left you without a guardian-redeemer. May he become famous throughout Israel! He will renew your life and sustain you in your old age. For your daughter-in-law, who loves you and who is better to you than seven sons, has given him birth. (4:14–15)

Let's take a step back and look at this story. Ruth did not go out and seek world peace (even though that is a wonderful endeavor). She simply decided to let her light shine on someone in her family. Her love and compassion for Naomi were the means that God used to change Naomi's life from one of loss to one of fullness and joy. And it did not stop there. The baby that Ruth had was the grandfather to King David, and Jesus came through that family line as well!

Just as it was for Ruth, when we decide to let our light shine on others, we have no idea how God will use our efforts to make an impact. But just as it was for Ruth, He can greatly exceed our expectations by letting that light spread further than anything we could ever dream of.

SHINING

So how can you and I let our lights shine in our daily lives? I don't think we need big grand gestures; we can start out small. Whatever tiny picture you have in your mind, shrink it even further, and maybe even further than that. Trust me. When I quit my first job, I was surprised that something that seemed incredibly tiny to me made a difference in other people's lives.

I'm a natural smiler, meaning I smile when I am happy, sad, frustrated, embarrassed, or basically any emotion. I am not sure why I do this—maybe many years of cheerleading—but more than once I have asked myself the question, *Why are you smiling while you are crying?* Anyway, my first job out of college was not the right fit for me, and I spent months trying to convince myself that I liked the work and stress of my job. I had to keep track of every six minutes of work I did, which meant taking bathroom breaks, getting coffee, and talking to coworkers did not count as working time. Since I was powering through, trying to prove myself as a good worker, it was hard to take a breath, talk to the people around me, and take the time away from billing to really love the people in my office.

There was one guy whose office was right across from mine. Every morning when he came in, I would look up from my pile of work, smile and say "good morning," then return to my way-too-intense work mode. Rarely did I ask questions or talk about anything because I was too focused on what I needed to get done. I felt guilty about not fostering that relationship, but my stress level was too high for me to change.

Fast-forward to the day I quit and went around the office telling people that I was leaving. I had the same conversation over and over, with people wishing me well, being surprised, or secretly smiling that they won the bet of how long the new person would last. When I got to my office neighbor and told him the news, I did not expect too strong of a reaction. I was just the person who sat in the office across from him. Instead, he told me that he was devastated because my smile was one thing that he looked forward to every day. I had no idea that such a small thing made a difference to him.

So, what little things can you do to let your light shine? To let other people see God's love through you? Can you bake cookies for your office for no reason, text a Bible passage you love to a friend, or simply smile at the person who walks past you in the grocery store (in a noncreepy way)?

Think about the friends, family members, or complete strangers who have surprised you and brightened your day. I think about my friend Edna from that same first job who was the Birthday Fairy. She uniquely decorated everyone's offices for their birthdays, including themes, piñatas, and rooms full of balloons. I think of my nieces and nephews who get giant smiles on their faces just because they see me, which always brightens my day. I think of the security guard at the airport who tells jokes with a completely straight face as I go through the metal detectors. I think of the baristas at my favorite coffee shop who always make a unique or interesting comment to me in the few moments while I am ordering. I think of the head of my math department in college who came to the coffee shop I studied at every single day with a new riddle for me. I think of my mom writing notes on my food as she packed my lunches for school each day. I think of the airline attendant who wrote down a list of book recommendations for me after seeing the book I was reading on the plane. I think of the owner of my favorite local donut shop who stops by every table to ask people how they are doing and remembers their answers. I think of my dad waking me up as a teenager by singing and dancing to my favorite songs. I think of the friends who check in, remembering that I had a big meeting or deadline. I think of the friend who takes the time to send me long, handwritten letters. The list could go on forever of all the people who have shined their light for me.

I am confident that you are already shining your light on many people, but imagine if you and I became a little more intentional with this in our lives. Imagine if it was our goal to let our lights shine to every person that crosses our paths—whether it is a childhood friend, a coworker, a family member, the repairperson, our annoying coworker, our insurance company, the bad drivers in the carpool lane, the person in line ahead of us, or a complete stranger walking beside us? What would it look like to notice all these people and let our lights shine on them?

That is how we can change the world: by caring about the people who are in our lives. Ruth cared about her mother-in-law, and God used Ruth to bring the Savior into the world through her descendants. Imagine what God can do with your light!

Who can you be a blessing to today? Think about the people you have known a long time: your close friends and family. Do they need your prayers? Can you write them a letter, deliver flowers, bring them coffee, call them, or invite them to play soccer?

Then think about the people you see regularly: your coworkers, the people at your church, or the people who have the same hobbies as you. Can you invite a new coworker to lunch, leave an anonymous gift for someone, or just take the time to really listen to what is going on in the lives of the people around you?

And lastly, think about the strangers who you have only a fleeting moment with and may never see again. How can you be an ambassador of God to them with a teensy-tiny amount of interaction? I think one of the greatest opportunities to shine is when something goes wrong. When your food order is wrong or the vet forgets to call you back, that is a huge opportunity to show what it means to follow Jesus. Respond with the grace God has given to you, not anger. When someone in line says something to you, put down your phone and start a conversation. Be present with people in each moment. Care about them, their problems, and what they are going through. Hold the door open for a stranger, help the young boy who seems lost, and seize every opportunity you can to show what it means to love the people around you.

VOLUNTEERING

Another great way to shine your light is through volunteering. God *loves* you and me. I find it so easy to minimize that statement. To forget that God specially chose me and wonderfully created me. To forget that He died for me. To forget that all my worries and problems will someday disappear when I see Jesus and get the biggest, most amazing hug from the God who has always been with me, taken care of me, and delighted in me. That day will come for each of us, and when I really spend time thinking about that wonderful future, it changes how I want to spend my present. I not only want to let my light shine to the people I encounter, I want to actively seek ways to reflect the joy God has filled me with in my community.

I want to live a life where I have the courage to step outside of my comfort zone, put aside my self-interest, and share God's love. You and I have an amazing opportunity to do that in our churches, in our communities, in our professions, and in so many places when we start looking. We can spend our time, resources, and talents making the world a better place by spreading God's love through volunteering.

I must admit that there are times in my life when I am very bad at volunteering. Even the word itself can make me a little uncomfortable or guilty. I think, *I am giving money to this cause so I don't need to do anything else.* Or I let my schedule get so full with work and fun that I have no time to spare. It takes time and effort to volunteer, and I would rather not commit to something when I am a busy person.

However, in my experience, the crazy thing about volunteering is that I normally get more out of it than what I put in. One of my favorite childhood memories is visiting the local nursing home with my mother. We would go, and my mother would read devotions to the residents. I still remember the names and faces of those people, the excitement I was filled with every time they showed me a new, colorful bird in the aviary, and how happy we were to visit and talk about God and our lives. It's been over twenty years and I still have those happy memories, along with ornaments on my Christmas tree that were willed to me by those friends that I will see again someday in heaven.

By volunteering to help move an older gentleman to a nursing home, I heard incredible stories of him fleeing for his life while doing mission work overseas. While making dinner for people with children in the hospital, I was inspired by the incredible character and hope of people suffering. While sorting shoes to go to Africa, I was reminded of how blessed I am to have so much more than I need. Volunteering has built my character, grown friendships, and helped me see how tiny my problems truly are compared to what is going on in the world.

HOW DO I VOLUNTEER?

As singles, we *typically* have the blessing of flexibility in our lives. I know that this is not true if you are in school or have an intense job or help take care of people. However, I have found that as a single, I can plan my nights and weekends however I want. I do not need to compromise or check in with anyone. As a result, I have a huge opportunity to use my time to volunteer. And although I would love to watch my favorite TV show, snuggle up with a good book, cook a delicious meal, or get drinks with a friend, none of those things come close to the memories and experiences I have had while serving others.

One of the great things about volunteering is that there are endless opportunities to help, making it easy to find something that is uniquely fit to our talents and interests. If we all cared only about saving the turtles, then we would forget about those experiencing homelessness, children in the foster care system, and the elderly.

Maybe you are already volunteering, but if you are feeling that nudge inside to go do something and you do not know what it is yet, I want to give you a few categories and ideas so you can start finding the perfect opportunity. As you read through the following ideas, jot down any thoughts that are sparked in your mind.

1. Community

Is there an opportunity or need in your community that piques your interest? It could be collecting food for a food pantry, cleaning up the trash to make your community more welcoming, loving fluffy animals at the humane society, mentoring kids through organizations like Big Brothers Big Sisters of America, volunteering as an election worker, giving care packages to those experiencing homelessness, or buying presents for families in need at Christmas.

2. Church

Is there a way you can serve at church? It could be teaching Sunday school, visiting people in the hospital or nursing home, starting a prayer group, leading a small group devotion, or making meals for families going through difficult times. Or maybe there is something you can do with your specific talents, like leading the choir or being like my mother who has stamped and crafted hundreds of cards for the church to use.

3. Professional

Are there any professional organizations that you can volunteer with? I am an engineer so I joined Engineers without Borders where I can volunteer my time to design projects and then go to developing countries to build water filtration systems, homes, wells, and other needed things. Have you heard of similar groups that relate to your profession?

You don't have to do something that relates to your career though. I am part of a few women's professional groups, and there are groups for many more hobbies and interests.

4. Causes

In the last chapter, we talked about what breaks your heart in this world that you want to do something about. Is there a cause that stirs you up and makes you want to help? For me, that cause is human trafficking. I cannot believe that something so terrible exists in this world, and I want to do whatever I can to fight it. Maybe for you it is raising money for medical research, taking better care of the earth, helping veterans, or mentoring at-risk children.

Once you have identified opportunities that seem like a good fit for you, think about how you want to go about getting involved. Sound scary? You do not have to volunteer alone. I have had so much fun getting a small group together at church to volunteer. Ask your friends or coworkers or family members to join you in this endeavor. Then, see what programs exist that you can volunteer through. Or think about starting your own so you can make it easier for others to help as well. You never know how much it will cause you to grow and learn.

I pray you've started thinking about the ways that you can start shining your light to the world. Think about them. Pray about them. Talk to friends about them. Then go out and make the world a better place. Show the world that you are an ambassador of God by spreading the love He has for the world. I cannot wait to see where it takes you and how God chooses to use you!

DIVING DEEPER

1. What characters in TV shows, movies, and books do you admire? Why do you admire them?

2. Why is saving the world more appealing than helping one person?

3. Can you think of biblical examples, other than Ruth, of people who let their light shine to those around them?

4. Who in your life is a good example of someone who serves others?

5. What prevents you from shining your light and volunteering?

6. What side effects come with helping others? See Matthew 5:16. Have you ever gotten something out of helping others?

7. What can you start doing today to be an ambassador of God to the people around you?

8. What volunteer opportunity are you going to start doing today?

afterword

YOU

I pray this is the beginning of a new way of living for you. Thanks for taking the time to journey through these many pages with me. You now have the tools to prosper, shine, and fight for peace and joy in the exact moment that you are living in. Remember, "You are the light of the world. A town built on a hill cannot be hidden" (Matt. 5:14).

It has taken me so long to learn the lessons I have written in these pages, and even though I know them now, that does not mean that I am magically living in perfect bliss every single moment of my life.

There are days when I am blinded by my struggles. I hit the snooze button for the tenth time as my cat pulls on my hair to feed him. And despite all that ruckus, I do not have the faintest desire to turn on the lights and get myself out of bed. I hope that staying under the covers will shield me from the truth that my life has not turned out the way I hoped it would.

There are times when I think I have finally found the right person for me and then just one small conversation completely destroys the hope I had slowly and reluctantly allowed myself to feel.

There are cold and lonely times in the middle of the freezing winter when I desperately long for someone to laugh with and stay warm beside.

There will be dark days and dark times as is natural in the ever-undulating waves and flow of our lives. But no matter how dark it gets, do not lose heart. You have a weapon to wield against the darkness, the fear, and the hopelessness. You have the truth. Listen to that whisper of hope that's telling you who you are and how much you matter to the only One who actually matters. God loves you with an everlasting love, and He is using every moment, including this one—including the darkest of moments—to build a future so glorious and hopeful that you would never be able to imagine it.

Let me leave you with one last story to really put your life into perspective. Let me tell you about my "first-world problems."

A few summers ago, I knocked off an item on my bucket list that would be written in large, all-capital letters and underlined if I actually kept a physical bucket list. I finally made it to Italy! I spent two weeks being spoiled with delicious food and wine, beautiful scenery, and adventures with my friends—such as literally sprinting through Naples with a pizza in my hands to not miss the last train back to Rome where we were staying. (We made it with three minutes to spare.)

After the tastes, laughter, and fun, the plane landed back home, and my life did a massive 180-degree turn from horseback riding through vineyards in Tuscany to finding my life in disarray. I travel pretty frequently for work, so I am accustomed to getting home from the airport to my clean house and my cat meowing up a storm as he looks at me out the window.

That is not what I came home to this time. As I was on my way back to the States, I read an email from my tenant that her fridge was no longer working, and when I went into my house, I found out that our fridges were apparently on strike together because mine was broken as well. Then I noticed a weird smell in my house. As I investigated, I found that my little kitty had decided to use the bathroom all over the place, which I later found out was due to a kidney stone. On top of that, there was another very bad smell in my kitchen. I opened the trash to find hundreds of maggots having a party. Gross. Not the warm welcome I had dreamed of (yes, I know—things could have been *much* worse).

Jet-lagged me was prepared to come home and pass out with a snuggly kitty, but that was no longer an option. In my distress, I thought, *Why can it not just be one thing? It always has to be everything at once!*

I have been through much worse than coming home from Italy to problems that YouTube, a cleaner home, and the vet can fix. I am sure you have been through much worse also. And there are so many stories of people going through numerous insanely hard things at once that my problems look like a speck of dust in comparison.

So let's focus on a group of people who have real stories of facing numerous horrible problems at once: the Israelites.

YOU THINK YOU'VE GOT PROBLEMS?

The Israelites were enjoying their lives in the promised land when all of a sudden, they had numerous enemies coming to fight them at the exact same time. First, they heard that one army was on their way to attack them, and then they got news that a second army was coming for them. To top it all off, a third army decided to approach at the exact same time. When it rains, it pours.

The Israelites knew that if they fought these three armies on their own, they had no chance of surviving. They knew this was beyond their abilities so they prayed a prayer to God that has become my mantra ever since I read this story. They said, "We do not know what to do, but our eyes are on you" (2 Chron. 20:12).

Welcome to every day of my life. At home, at work, with friends, and *especially* in dealing with singleness—"God, I do not know what to do, but my eyes are on You."

After they had prayed this prayer, God did not tell the Israelites how He was going to save them. He did not lay out every single detail of their path so they could have the full comfort of knowing how and why they would be OK. Instead, He told them this: "Do not be afraid or discouraged because of this vast army. For the battle is not yours but God's. . . . Go out to face them tomorrow, and the LORD will be with you" (vv. 15–17).

So, not knowing how they would be saved but trusting that God was with them and would fight for them, they marched out to face the three armies. As they were marching, what do you think they were thinking? Were they cowering in fear of what would come? Were they feeling sorry for themselves and the situation they were in? Were they hopeless as to what would happen next?

No! As they marched out, they decided to confidently go with faith and trust in God, to such an extent that they actually sang praises to God as they marched. They sang, "Give thanks to the LORD, for his love endures forever" (v. 21).

So what happened then? As the Israelites were marching into battle and singing praises to God, the three armies assembled. God caused them not to wait for the Israelites to get to the battleground but to attack one another. First, two of the armies decided to be friends and ganged up to destroy the third army. Then the first two armies decided their friendship was over and destroyed one another. By the time the Israelites got to the battlefield, all that was left were the dead bodies of the three armies. No one had escaped. The God the Israelites trusted in had done more than they could have ever imagined.

We have no idea what our single lives will bring—the darkness, the length of this life stage, the depth of our loneliness. Every day, we are walking into the unknown. Just like it appeared for the Israelites, our situation can look significantly worse before it looks better. But do you want to live your life in fear—fear that you will never meet someone, fear that you will never be happy again, fear that you will get hurt—or do you want to be like the Israelites and march into the battle of your life belting out praises to God because you know that whatever you face, God will get you through it?

You are living in your moment right here and now with the Maker of the stars and universe ready to help and guide you. Where will your path lead? What will you do? Only you can make the choice to step out in full trust of the love that God has for you. I pray that you continue to shine through every trial that comes your way. Remember the big picture and what your eternity will bring. Remember who is with you.

The God who fought the battle for the Israelites is the God who is sitting next to you right now. This is the God who is listening intently to what you have to say with perfect understanding of how you feel. This is the God who is with you step by step in every place you have ever been and every place you will ever go. You have the perfect love of the most loving, powerful, and perfect being that has ever existed. This is where you belong. ♥

"I have loved you with an everlasting love."

Jeremiah 31:3

acknowledgments

To God: No amount of thanks can possibly come close to what You have done for me. Thank You for blowing my mind in what You do in my life every single day.

To Jeremy and Megume Treuden: This book would not have happened without your friendship and love. Thank you for having your hearts beat with mine in my dreams. Thank you for the many brainstorms and for constantly uplifting me in my single life. Thank you for the graphic designs, the branding, the photos, and being with me in every moment from the whisper of an idea to the final book.

To Josh Grefe: Thank you for your constant encouragement and confidence in my book as this process brought out my insecurities and fears. Thank you for reminding me to enjoy and feel blessed in every step of the journey.

To my parents, Tom and Chris Schermerhorn: Thank you for living out your passion for God my entire life and for your overwhelming support in this dream of mine.

To Charis Scharf: Thank you for encouraging me, being an inspiring single, and still being willing to fix my grammar after all these years.

To Leslie (Wochos) Koenig: Thank you for believing in me as an author before I ever tried to write a book. Those days of dreaming up other worlds while we rode on the bus before singing in churches sparked my creativity to start writing. Thank you for your wisdom and your ability to always help me take a breath and enjoy life.

To Maggie Hall: Thank you for always listening to my ideas (including some very rough early ideas for this book) and encouraging me in my creativity. I'm your little sister and have always wanted to be like you, so thank you for being such a great example.

To Josh, Becky, Penny, Jack, Otto, and Tessa Schermerhorn and Lawton Hall: Thank you for being my amazing family members who make me smile, help my creativity, and support me in my many endeavors.

To the people who got this book published: Thank you, Bethany Vredeveld, for sharing my project with Pastor Bruce Becker who introduced me to Jason Jones at Jones Literary who gave my proposal to my agent, Macey Howell. Macey Howell, I could not ask for a better agent. Thank you so much for taking my dream and making it come true! I am so blessed to have you!

To Rebekah Guzman at Baker, for believing in this book. You brought about one of the happiest moments of my life when I found out this book was getting published! To Robin Turici, thank you for your editorial magic. To the entire team at Baker: Thank you so much for publishing this book and getting it into people's hands!

To Jamie Chavez: Thank you for being a wonderful editor to this first-time author.

To my early draft readers, including Elizabeth Larson, Stanley Chan, Dan Kemnitz, Emily Buch, and Kayla Scott: Thank you for reading through my terrible spelling to give me great feedback and boost my confidence.

Thank you to Pastor Jason Ewart for adding incredible depth to my understanding of God's Word. So many of these pages have been influenced by your sermons.

Thank you to my church family who has been encouraging me and praying for me for years: Jeff and Annette Timm, Kristina and Dan Magsig, Charisse and Dan Moldenhaur, Linda and Rick Kraemer, Scott and Andrea Huedepohl, Brittany and Eric Broman, and Pat Weiss.

Thank you to all the friends who listened to me and supported me in my writing, including my work wife, Lorraine Wong; the best mentor in the entire world, Kyle Crum; my Book Proposal Bootcamp buddy, Meghan Mellinger; as well as Jessie Skaer, Beth Kraemer, Heidi Brody, Kim Joerres, Christa Fierros, Jake Caya, Jenna Swanson, Turner Swanson, Jessica Peters, Katie Richardson, and Allie Keller.

To all the people who have been praying for me, following me, and encouraging me: Thank you for constantly reminding me why I am doing this.

And to you who read my book: A huge thank-you! I pray that God has filled you with joy and hope while reading these pages.

Hannah Schermerhorn lives in Milwaukee, Wisconsin, with her cat, Fritz. She is an electrical engineer who has worked in legal, business, and global marketing. Hannah enjoys traveling, reading, and spending time with her nieces and nephews. You can follow Hannah on Facebook and Instagram @onlyasinglelife or on hannahschermerhorn.com.

Connect
WITH HANNAH

Whether you are dealing with loneliness, are living your life to the fullest, or find yourself somewhere in between, Hannah wants to connect with you! Visit HannahSchermerhorn.com to meet a vibrant online community and sign up for regular updates from the author.

Connect with

BakerBooks

Relevant. Intelligent. Engaging.

Sign up for announcements about
new and upcoming titles at

BakerBooks.com/SignUp

@ReadBakerBooks

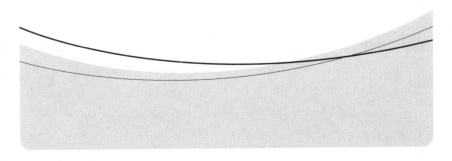